The Book of MICROWAVE COOKERY

The Book of MICROWAVE COOKERY
Sonia Allison

David & Charles
Newton Abbot   London   North Pomfret (Vt)
in association with Thorn Domestic Appliances
(Electrical) Ltd

British Library Cataloguing in Publication Data

Allison, Sonia
  The book of microwave cookery
  1. Microwave cookery
  I. Title
  641.5'88   TX832
  ISBN 0-7153-7525-3

Library of Congress Catalog Card Number 77-91467

First published 1978
Second impression 1978
Third impression 1980

© Sonia Allison 1978

Printed in Great Britain by
A. Wheaton & Co. Limited Exeter
for David & Charles (Publishers) Limited
Brunel House Newton Abbot Devon

Published in the United States of America
by David & Charles Inc
North Pomfret Vermont 05053 USA

To my scientific husband, for his
constructive advice and guidance; to my
son, for eating the food as fast as I could
cook it; to my mother, for washing up.

Contents

Preface **6**

Introduction: the microwave oven **7**

Microwaves **7**

How and why microwave energy cooks food **8**

Arrangement of food in the oven **8**

Standing or resting times **8**

Safety precautions **9**

Cleaning **9**

Seasoning your cooking **9**

Suitable utensils for use in the microwave **9**

Ceramic browning dishes or skillets **12**

Types of microwave oven **12**

Input and output **12**

Pulsing **13**

Use of the power control dial **13**

Appearance of microwave-cooked foods **16**

Advantages of a microwave oven **16**

But a few reminders **17**

1 Snacks, convenience meals, eggs and cheese **18**

Convenience food chart **18**

Recipes **24**

2 Starters **31**

3 Soups **38**

4 Fish **42**

Fish defrosting and cooking guide **42**

Recipes **43**

5 Meat and poultry **47**

Defrosting meat and poultry **47**

Defrosting times **48**

Defrosting times for an oven with a defrost switch or power control dial **48**

Cooking meat and poultry **50**

Meat and poultry 'roasting' chart **50**

Recipes **51**

6 Vegetables **70**

Cooking fresh vegetables **70**

Cooking times **72**

Frozen vegetables **74**

Recipes **74**

7 Rice and pasta **80**

8 Sauces **84**

9 Puddings **90**

Defrosting frozen fruit **90**

Fresh fruit cooking chart **90**

Recipes **91**

10 Cakes **100**

Recipes **102**

11 Yeast mixtures **109**

12 Confectionery **113**

13 Preserves **116**

14 Combination dishes **120**

15 Hints and tips **125**

Acknowledgements **125**

Index **127**

Preface

When I was first confronted with a microwave and began cooking the simplest of things—beans on toast or even scrambled eggs—I confess that its rapidity of action filled me with a measure of trepidation. I felt like a toddler taking its first steps into the unknown. How on earth could a cake cook in four minutes, a Christmas pudding in six, a beef curry in twenty-five and hollandaise sauce in seconds? Why did food never stick to the dishes? How come the kitchen was always cool, despite a mammoth microwave cook-in in the height of summer? Why did everything taste so much fresher? Why did our fuel bills show an appreciable drop? Was my imagination playing tricks or was a microwave oven one of the most advanced and revolutionary pieces of kitchen equipment this century had ever seen? The answers came thick and fast. Within weeks, I discovered—in common with caterers who have been using these ovens successfully and as a matter of course for a good number of years—that a microwave was ultra-fast by nature, reliable, hygienic, safe and extremely economical on fuel. It was simple to operate and even more simple to use, easily transportable from room to room, and for the most part, attractive to look at. Its limitations were few. Not only would it reheat leftovers and defrost and cook frozen foods in the briefest space of time, but I had endless possibilities of cooking sumptuous meals with the minimum of effort and the maximum of speed. For the first time in a long time, day-to-day cooking was fun and, because it was fun, completely relaxing. As confidence grew, family interest developed and without a hint of a grumble, my husband and son volunteered to cook dinner for *me* because, they said, 'It doesn't take long in the microwave'.

The two hundred or so recipes in this book have all been personally tried and tested. They represent a cross-section of old favourites with a sprinkling of new ideas and, when appropriate, I have deliberately included conventionally difficult dishes which, in a microwave, are greatly simplified: just look at the Yeast Mixtures section and some of the sauces, for example. Introductions to sections and the relative charts should clarify queries relating to different recipes and foods, and I would ask you to follow closely the section on suitable utensils for use in the microwave. As it is helpful to know how a piece of equipment works and why, I shall begin on that note and hopefully iron out some of the problems confronting new owners of microwave cookers, those who already have one but are still perplexed through lack of information, and those who are debating whether or not to buy one.

Sonia Allison

One of the greatest joys of my life is a microwave oven, because it has given me the very thing I needed above all else: extra leisure time. With a heavy and demanding job, a home to run and a family to care for, relaxation has always been a much appreciated value-added bonus and, like many woman in my position, preparing and cooking an evening meal night after night with relentless regularity, providing unexpected and hefty teas for packs of hungry boys as they come ploughing through the door after school, entertaining friends and colleagues—all these, as my workload increased, became a burdensome, irritating and time-consuming chore instead of a pleasurable, satisfying and creative occupation. I longed for almost anything to take some of the load off my shoulders and then, out of the blue, a microwave oven dropped into my lap and my whole pattern of life suddenly changed. I found, to my absolute delight, that I could prepare dinner—and a three-course one at that—in well under an hour; I could produce enough substantial eats in twenty minutes to sate the ferocious appetites of those seemingly insatiable youngsters; and, with the minimum of forward planning, I could lay on a feast of a meal in well under two hours for the most critical and discriminating of guests. It was, and still is, almost too good to be true and the more I work with the microwave, the more I value and admire its adaptability, the more devoted I become to it and the more grateful I am for its existence.

Although a microwave oven is habit-forming, I have to admit in all honesty that microwaving is not entirely the be-all and end-all of my thinking. I still have to use a conventional cooker for the few things it cannot cope with—Yorkshire pudding, pancakes, meringues, éclairs, soufflés, scones, crisp pastry and hard eggs—but I have manipulated the microwave to suit my own needs and, over the months, tested a repertoire of recipes which has proved to me that this small, work-top box of an oven is even more versatile in its performance than I imagined or expected it to be.

Introduction

If you buy a conventional cooker, dishwasher, freezer or washing machine, the chances are that you will accept the technical side without too many questions, knowing that competent engineers and designers have taken a great deal of time and trouble to produce a machine which is functional, does a good job and gives satisfactory service. But as microwave ovens are comparatively new world-wide and are attracting an enormous amount of interest, a short explanation of their behaviour seems justified.

Microwaves

Microwaves or microwave energy—on which the principle of radar is based—are electromagnetic, short-length, high-frequency radio waves at the top end of the radio band. They are close to, but not as powerful as, infra-red rays. The frequency is 2450 MHz or megahertz which means millions of cycles or vibrations per second. (The term 'hertz' is in recognition of Heinrich Hertz, the German scientist, who first detected electromagnetic waves.)

Obviously the waves are in no way harmful and are very far removed from the dangerous rays that alarm people: X-rays, gamma-rays, and ultra-violet rays, which are known to cause damaging cellular changes. *Microwaves do not*, and of equal importance, they are non-cumulative. Even if one were, accidentally, exposed to microwaves, the worst that could happen would be a nasty burn. Browning oneself under a sun lamp, sunbathing in the direct glare of the sun for hours on end, subjecting oneself to too much do-it-yourself infra-red treatment for rheumatic conditions —all these are infinitely more dangerous than using a microwave oven. Each oven has to conform to strict statutory safety standards laid down in every country. Modern technology has ensured that these ovens are as safe as possible, cut-out devices are automatically built in and when once the oven door is opened, the microwave energy immediately switches off. Rarely is there a microwave 'leak' although this could occur if the door seal were faulty (it is advisable to check periodically) or if, through neglect and lack of service, the hinges had rusted. In the unlikely event of the see-through glass or plastic front fracturing, *do not use the oven*, but contact a service engineer as soon as possible.

How and why microwave energy cooks food

Microwave energy is emitted from a device called a magnetron which is generally situated at the top of the oven, usually towards one side, and shielded by a plastic cover. As the microwaves, transmitted down a channel called a waveguide, enter the cooking cavity (inside of oven), they bounce off the metal sides and 'beam' on to the food from all directions. Simultaneously the microwaves become absorbed by the food and thus force the water molecules within the food itself to vibrate at a hectic rate—around 2400 million cycles or vibrations per second. This creates rapid friction and, in turn, the friction creates enough heat to cook whatever is inside the oven fast and efficiently. For a simple comparison, rub your hands briskly together and notice how warm they become. Then imagine millions of you all doing the same thing at the same time. A terrific amount of heat would be generated. Microwaves work in the same way and although they are incapable of actually cooking the food, they shake it up to such an extent that the heat generated from within does the work and the food cooks itself in a fraction of the time it would take if cooked conventionally.

The stirrer blade (sometimes called a paddle) or fan, also housed at the top or side of the oven, distributes the microwave energy uniformly throughout the oven and prevents what are commonly called hot and cold spots, which would result in uneven cooking.

Arrangement of food in the oven

I explained earlier that microwaves are short-length, high-frequency radio waves. Short is the operative word here because the waves are capable of penetrating only 2½cm (1in) of the food all the way round and from top to bottom. Therefore a plate or dish of food could well stay cool in the middle, while the outside edges heat unless treated correctly. For this reason, food should be stirred (edges to centre) where indicated in a specific recipe or chart. Similarly, cakes and rolls, buns, jacket potatoes, etc, should be of equal size for preference, and should be arranged in a circle either on the base of the oven itself, or on a plate in the oven. Complete meals on plates should be so arranged that the food is distributed in an even layer.

Standing or resting times

You will find either of these two terms mentioned throughout the book. What the 'stop and start' action is all about is simply this. When once food has finished its cooking cycle, it goes on cooking for some time as the heat continues its journey from the outside of the food to the middle (by conduction). Because of this, some recipes are not stirred but are left to stand and literally 'stew in their own juices'.

Anyone who has had anything to do with a microwave oven always gives the same advice: *undercook rather than overcook*. Food can always be cooked for a few seconds or minutes longer but when once it has dried out—and this can happen very quickly—there is no remedial treatment. With a cake, for example, it is best to take it out of the oven while the top is still fractionally moist and then leave it to stand (inside or outside the oven, whichever suits you) until cooking is complete. Similarly, to prevent frozen food cooking round the edges before the centre has thawed, it should be given, manually, so many minutes energy and so many minutes rest. (The manual side does not apply where there is an automatic defrost setting.) Food can be left to stand, after cooking is completed, inside or outside the oven, whichever is most convenient.

Safety precautions

Never switch on an empty microwave oven. If there is no food to absorb the microwaves, they bounce back to the magnetron and shorten its life. To be on the safe side, always keep a glass or cup of water standing in the empty oven in case it gets switched on by accident. The same applies when heating small amounts of food, and if, for example, you are melting a tablespoon or two of butter, leave the glass or cup of water in the oven.

Cleaning

Keep walls, top and base of oven clean by wiping over with a damp cloth immediately after use. Leftover splashes are not only hard to remove, but also absorb some of the microwave energy. This reduces efficiency and puts up fuel costs.

Seasoning your cooking

Minimal salt should be used in microwave cooking as it has a toughening effect, especially on meat and poultry. Seasoning should be adjusted at the end of the cooking time.

Suitable utensils for use in the microwave

Microwaves behave differently according to what they are hitting. If they beam on to metal, they are reflected. If they beam on to glass, pottery, porcelain, china, plastic and paper, they are transmitted in a similar way to sunlight passing through a window. If the microwaves beam on to anything containing liquid (and this applies to practically all foods), they are absorbed. Bearing this in mind, it is essential to use the correct cooking utensils in a microwave oven for successful results. Equally important is knowing what *not* to use. The following are all ideal for use in a microwave oven because they do not obstruct the passage of microwaves to the food; in other words, the microwaves are able to pass directly through the utensil, enabling the food to cook but not heating the utensil itself to any great extent.

Glass

Any type of glass utensil is satisfactory, provided it has no metal trim. Thus you can use Pyrex-type dishes, glass jugs, tumblers, plates and measuring cups. Ceramic glass dishes, such as Pyroflam, respond extremely well to microwave cooking.

Pottery and china (porcelain)

Either can be used, provided there is no metal trim. Pottery which contains non-visible pieces of metal slows down cooking. So do dark dishes and both kinds will be fairly hot to the touch.

Plastic

If of the rigid kind, this can be used satisfactorily in a microwave oven. It does, however, absorb more microwave energy than glass, pottery, china and porcelain and will therefore be hotter to the touch. *Do not be tempted into using lightweight plastic containers* such as empty yogurt or cottage-cheese cartons as the heat from the food will cause them to melt.

Breakfast dishes   Scrambled eggs, mushrooms, tomatoes and bacon; both eggs and bacon cook extremely well in a microwave oven, bacon with less shrinkage than when cooked in a conventional oven. (Recipe page 24)

Cling wrap

This is excellent both for lining dishes and for covering. When used as a cover, it is inclined to stretch and 'balloon-up' during cooking and for this reason, I have suggested slitting it with scissors in those recipes where it is recommended.

Roasting bags

Using roasting bags is an extremely convenient and clean method of cooking a variety of foods and the resultant flavour, colour and texture are excellent. Browning takes place more readily in roasting bags and they are well worth using for 'roasting' joints of meat and poultry. The metal ties provided with the roasting bags should not be used. Good substitutes are elastic bands or a thin string tie.

Plastic spatulas and wooden spoons

These may be used for stirring and can be left in the dish while the food is cooking.

Baskets and wooden bowls

Brief spells in the microwave will do no harm but prolonged cooking will cause dryness and loss of shape.

Paper

To keep the floor of the oven clean and to absorb a certain amount of moisture, foods can be stood on ordinary paper towels before cooking. If used as a cover, paper towels prevent spluttering. Greaseproof paper (American wax paper) can also be used but it works out more expensive than paper towels.

Waxed paper and waxed plates

These may be used but only briefly, as prolonged heating will cause the wax to melt.

Metal

In general, metal pots and pans and other utensils with a high proportion of metal should *not be used at all in the microwave*. The two main reasons are:

1 The metal acts as a barrier and prevents the microwaves reaching the food. Therefore it will not cook.
2 Any metal object in the cooking cavity causes arcing, which resembles miniature flashes of lightning. This is damaging to the magnetron. Also, it can ruin metal trims on crockery. In this context, always look underneath a cup or saucer, etc, because if there is a gold or silver maker's mark it too could cause arcing.

There are certain exceptions to the use of metal in a microwave. Metal skewers used for a dish such as kebabs are safe enough, provided the metal does not go near the sides, top or base of the oven and the skewers themselves are densely packed with food. Here the metal is inside the food and not the food inside the metal; thus no arcing should occur.

Sometimes foil can be used safely. Indeed, to prevent wings of poultry and thin parts of joints from becoming overcooked, they should be protected with a close, smooth covering of foil. The foil will cause no damage because it is used in small quantities, and because the proportion of food far exceeds that of foil.

Never ever place an opened can of food to heat in a microwave oven. Always transfer the contents to a plate or dish.

Ceramic browning dishes or skillets

These are ceramic dishes which are especially designed to absorb microwave energy and brown food at the same time. They are preheated in the microwave oven and then the food to be cooked is placed inside. The hot surface immediately sears the surface of the food—like a grill—while the microwave energy cooks the food. They are excellent for cooking steaks, chops, sausages, etc.

Types of microwave oven

A microwave oven closely resembles a TV set in size and appearance, though it is not as deep and the dials are fewer. The internal capacity is less than one imagines at first glance but all except the smallest-sized microwave will take up to a $5\frac{1}{2}$kg (12lb) turkey.

There are basically five types of microwave oven.
1 Those with only a minute timer-dial and a power push button.
2 Those with minute and second timer-dials together with a power push button.
3 As No 2 but also with a pulsing unit. This means that when required (for defrosting for example) the oven will switch itself on and off automatically for so many seconds at a time. (More details later in this section.)
4 Those fitted with a power control dial numbered 1 to 7 (see page 13 for details). Some of these cookers have no numbers, but written against the dial instead are the appropriate settings for the type of food being cooked. Thus Moffat's No 6 would equate in general terms to reheating precooked foods, cooking minced beef and fish, roasting chickens, poaching fruit and cooking vegetables, etc.
5 Those like Nos 3 and/or 4 but with either a browning element, a rotating turntable (to eliminate turning dishes), and/or a stirrer blade, and/or a 'keep warm' setting which does exactly as it says: keeps cooked foods warm.

The choice is very much dependent on how much you want to spend (obviously sophisticated cookers with every gimmick and gadget are more expensive than the simpler models) and also how much you want your oven to do.

Input and output

The majority of microwave ovens consume an input of 1000 to 1500 watts of electricity with corresponding outputs of 500 to 700 watts. The output is the magnetron power which controls the amount of microwave energy used in a specific oven. All the recipes in this book are based on a 600 watt output. If you are unsure of the output of your own particular model, a simple comparison test can be made by heating 150ml or 1½dl (¼pt or American ⅝ cup) tap water until it boils. The average time should be about 2¼ minutes. If it boils more quickly, it may mean the output is higher than 600 watts (maybe 650) and cooking time of recipes should be reduced accordingly; similarly, if the water takes longer to boil, the cooking times should be slightly increased. Although the wattage output is the controlling factor in cooking, the total input of electricity is used by the magnetron, stirrer blade and cooling fan, the power converter and the interior and pilot lights.

Pulsing

A pulse control—sometimes referred to as a defrost switch—turns the microwave power on and off automatically every so many seconds, eg fifteen seconds on and fifteen seconds off, thirty seconds on and thirty seconds off and so on. In this way, foods are given short bursts of microwave energy with rests in between. While resting, the heat distributes itself through the food and overcooking is avoided. This technique is especially useful for defrosting foods, such as poultry and meat, prior to cooking.

Power control dial

The power control dial feature on some microwave ovens provides more flexibility and control of the cooking speed.

Some foods, such as the less expensive cuts of meat and poultry, need slower cooking to help tenderise them. Slower cooking also allows food flavours to blend more thoroughly in such dishes as meat sauces and curries.

When a setting between 1 and 6 on the power control dial has been selected, the microwave energy in the oven cycles on and off at varying rates, depending on the setting chosen. At setting such as 'low' 1, 2 and 3,

the energy is off for longer than it is on. At 'defrost—setting 4—the microwave energy on-time and off-time will be approximately the same. As the control is moved on to settings 5 and 6, the energy is on for longer than it is off. At 'normal' setting 7, the energy is on all the time.

Use of the power control dial

'Low' Setting 1
Energy on for approximately 25 per cent of the time.
Use for:
1 Keeping foods warm for about ½ hour or less.
2 Softening butter, cream cheese, proving yeast doughs, melting chocolate, and melting method cake mixtures.

Setting 2
Energy on for approximately 30 per cent of the time.
Use for:
1 Finishing off casseroles, stews and meat sauces which have been first cooked on setting 7 for half the cooking time. Food flavours and seasonings will blend better during this slower cooking stage.

Setting 3
Energy on for approximately 40 per cent of the time.
Use for:
1 Cooking soft custards and egg-based custards.
2 Cooking less tender cuts of meat.

'Defrost' Setting 4
Energy on for approximately 50 per cent of the time.
Use for:
1 Thawing foods, eg meat, poultry, fish.

Setting 5
Energy on for approximately 60 per cent of the time.
Use for:
1 Cooking yeast doughs.
2 Pâtés.
3 Cooking pasta and rice after water has boiled on 'normal' setting 7.

Pizza   Ideal for snack lunches and suppers. The microwave will speed the proving of the dough and the final pizza will cook in five minutes. (Recipe page 111)

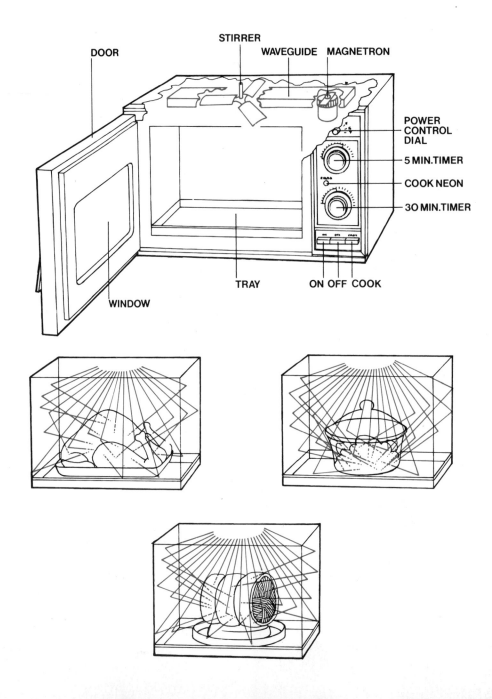

STIRRER

DOOR   WAVEGUIDE   MAGNETRON

POWER
CONTROL
DIAL

5 MIN. TIMER

COOK NEON

30 MIN. TIMER

TRAY   ON OFF COOK

WINDOW

Setting 6

Energy on for approximately 75 per cent of the time. Use for:

1 Reheating most precooked foods, eg sliced meat, canned foods, entrées, fish, pasta and rice.
2 Roasting less tender joints for half the cooking time and then completing the rest of cooking on setting 3.
3 Cooking minced beef, fish.
4 Roasting chickens.
5 Poaching fruit, cooking vegetables.

'Normal' Setting 7

Energy on for 100 per cent of the time. Most foods can be cooked at this setting and the bulk of the recipes in this book have been tested on the equivalent to 'normal' setting 7.

Appearance of microwave-cooked foods

In general, foods cooked in a microwave do not take on that rich golden colour associated with baking and grilling in a conventional oven. In many instances this matters not at all, or can be overcome by using brown gravy cubes in meat and poultry dishes, and coating tops of cakes with icing sugar or icing. However, prolonged cooking in a microwave will bring about some browning, especially of meat and poultry. To encourage browning even further, you can sprinkle joints of meat or poultry with paprika before cooking or brush over with basting sauce (see Sauces section). Using roasting bags for cooking also helps the food to brown.

Advantages of a microwave oven

1 Speed. It saves an average of 50 to 75 per cent of normal cooking time.
2 It is approximately four times as efficient as cooking conventionally. As all the energy is directed to the food there is no 'over-spill' into the oven cavity or kitchen.
3 Economy. Depending on how much you cook, a microwave oven can save up to 50 per cent of your electric cooking-fuel bill.

4   No preheating of a microwave oven is necessary.

5   Coolness. When you cook, you will notice that the interior walls of the oven, the utensils used, and the kitchen itself all stay cool. The only piping hot thing will be the food.

6   Cooking odours are largely contained and do not obtrude.

7   Fast defrosting. This can be a tremendous help to working women and to those confronted by unexpected guests. Also, as cooking time is so short, meal planning can be more versatile and spontaneous.

8   Cleanliness. Because the interior of the oven never gets hot, spattered food and spills do not bake on and can very easily be removed with a damp cloth. For extra speed, put a cup of water in the oven and heat it up. The steam it produces will moisten the oven, and a quick wipe over with paper towels will clean it up.

9   Less washing up. Firstly, you can cook and heat in oven-to-table glass or pottery casseroles and so use fewer dishes; secondly, nothing bakes on, nor sticks to, the dish so with a quick wash, it is as good as new.

10   You can speed up *all* your cooking by using a conventional cooker with a microwave oven. Bread can be baked about eight minutes in a microwave and finished off conventionally in ten minutes. A 'combination' pie—and you will find a selection in the Combination Dishes section—will take maybe thirty minutes instead of an hour.

11   It reheats perfectly. If members of the family return home at odd hours or in relays, you can reheat plates of refrigerated lunch or dinner in a matter of minutes. The food tastes as though it has been freshly cooked and does not dry out as it would if reheated in a conventional oven; nor will harmful germs on cold, cooked meat multiply as they do in the warmth of a moderate oven.

12   If you have some free time and feel creative, a microwave enables you to have a massive 'cook-in'. All the food can be deep frozen and then defrosted and reheated in the microwave when needed.

13   Foods cooked in a microwave oven have a clear colour and a fresher flavour than those cooked conventionally. (Taste some frozen peas and a chicken if you need convincing.) Also, because of the speed of cooking, less valuable nutrients are lost.

14   There is less shrinkage of foods when they are cooked in a microwave which makes for economy.

15   Provided the timer is correctly set, there is no danger of overcooking because the microwave automatically switches itself off with, in some instances, an audible warning.

16   Because the kitchen is not subjected to so much steam, the walls, ceilings and fitments will keep cleaner longer.

But a few reminders

1   You cannot brown food in the microwave to the same extent as in a conventional oven or under the grill.

2   A microwave oven is not recommended for cooking Yorkshire pudding (it goes flat), pancakes, meringues, éclairs, soufflés, scones, crisp pastry, hard eggs and rich cakes made by the creaming method. Some of these dishes can, however, be reheated satisfactorily in a microwave.

3   You have to re-think utensils completely and forget about using metal pots nnd pans. This means you either have to improvise with what you already have (for example, standing a tumbler in the middle of a glass dish if making a ring cake instead of using a ring tin or mould) or invest in new dishes.

4   The cooking times given for all recipes in this book are intended as a guide only, since the amount of microwave energy required differs according to the sizes and types of dishes used, the temperature of the food at the commencement of cooling, and the depth of the food in the dish.

1 Snacks

Cheesy baked beans on toast   Delicious for hungry children in a hurry and a good 'trial run' as you begin to use your microwave. (Recipe page 25)

The recipes in this section are useful as a trial run for beginners, and those who have just acquired a microwave oven are well advised to acquaint themselves with it by trying out the easiest things first such as cocoa, porridge, bacon, beans on toast, rarebits and scrambled eggs. As success comes, so will the desire to go on to bigger and better things such as omelets and fondues.

The Convenience Food Chart (prepared by Valerie Collins of Thorn) shows how you should best handle an assortment of frozen, canned and packeted foods, and freezer owners should find it a helpful and informative guide.

Convenience food chart

Food	Metric and American	Time to thaw	Time to cook	Comments
Frozen meats				
12oz frozen gravy and roast beef Remove from foil tray and place on serving dish.	350g 12oz	Heat 3 minutes. Leave to stand for 3 minutes.	$3\frac{1}{2}$ minutes	
4oz frozen gravy and roast beef Remove from foil tray and place on serving dish.	125g 4oz	Heat 2 minutes. Leave to stand for 2 minutes.	$1\frac{1}{2}$ minutes	
4 large frozen pork or beef sausages	4 large 4 large	Heat 1 minute— separate. Heat 1 minute. Leave to stand for 2 minutes.	6 minutes	Place sausages on plate. Cover with kitchen paper to stop spluttering.
2 Pork chops, frozen	2 medium 2 medium	Heat 2 minutes. Leave to stand for 2 minutes.	3 minutes	Cover during cooking.
$\frac{1}{2}$lb Lamb's liver, frozen	225g 8oz	Heat 2 minutes. Leave to stand for 5 minutes.	3 minutes	Cover during cooking.
13oz Chicken joint, frozen	375g 13oz	Heat $1\frac{1}{2}$ minutes. Leave to stand for 5 minutes. Heat further $1\frac{1}{2}$ minutes.	5 minutes	Cook in roasting bag.

Food	Metric and American	Time to thaw	Time to cook	Comments
¼lb Mince, frozen	225g 8oz ground beef	Heat 1½ minutes. Leave to stand for 5 minutes. Heat 1 minute.		Scrape off edges of mince as it thaws, so that centre defrosts more quickly.
1lb Mince, frozen	½kg 16oz ground beef	Heat 1½ minutes. Leave to stand for 5 minutes. Heat 1½ minutes. Leave to stand for 5 minutes.		Scrape off edges of mince as it thaws, so that centre defrosts more quickly.
2 x 5oz Lamb chops, frozen	each 150g each 5oz	Heat 2 minutes. Leave to stand for 2 minutes.	2 minutes	Cover during cooking.
¼lb Bacon, frozen	225g 8oz bacon slices or strips.	Heat 2 minutes. Leave to stand for 8 minutes	Cook 3 minutes. Turn. Cook further 2½ minutes.	Cover with paper towels.
8 Pork chipolatas, frozen	8 8	Heat 2 minutes. Leave to stand for 2 minutes.	Cook 3 minutes. Turn. Cook further 3 minutes.	Cover with paper towels.
Frozen fish 2 x 3½oz Fish steaks, frozen	each 90g each 3½ oz	Heat 3½ minutes. Leave to stand for 5 minutes.	Cook 3 minutes. Turn. Cook further 3 minutes.	After thawing, cover with cling film to prevent drying.
7½oz buttered smoked haddock ('Boil-in-Bag'), frozen	215g 7½oz		6 minutes	Slit top of bag crossways before cooking for ease of serving.
10 Fish fingers, frozen	10 fish fingers 10 fish sticks	Heat 4 minutes. Leave to stand 2 minutes.	4 minutes	Dot with butter before cooking.
2 x 2oz Fish cakes	each 50g each 2oz	Heat 2½ minutes. Leave to stand for 3 minutes.	1 minute	
Other frozen savouries Frozen individual pies (Remove from foil dish and put in serving dish.)	Frozen individual pies Frozen individual pies	Heat 1½ minutes. Leave to stand for 2 minutes. Brush with milk.	Cook 1½ minutes. Turn. Cook 1½ minutes.	Pies tend to lose shape during cooking.
8oz Frozen pizza	225g 8oz		Cook 2½ minutes. Turn. Cook 2½ minutes.	Cover with paper towels to prevent spluttering.

Food	Metric and American	Time to thaw	Time to cook	Comments
14oz Shepherds pie, frozen (remove from foil container and put in dish.)	400g 14oz	Heat 5 minutes. Leave to stand for 2 minutes.	6 minutes	Brown top under hot grill if desired.
16oz Lasagne, frozen (remove from foil container and put in dish.)	½kg 16oz	Heat 4 minutes. Leave to stand for 3 minutes. Heat further 3 minutes.	9 minutes	Cover with paper towels to prevent spluttering.
Canned foods				
Creamed rice pudding (15½oz can)	440g 15½oz		Cook 3 minutes, stirring once.	Cover
Soya type casserole chunks (15½oz tin)	440g 15½oz		Cook 2 minutes. Stir well. Cook 2 minutes.	Cover
Canned reconstituted condensed soup 2 x ½pt mugs	575ml 20 fluid oz		Cook 3 minutes. Stir well. Cook 2 minutes. Stir well. Cook 3 minutes.	See Soup section.
Tinned pasta 15½oz can Spaghetti hoops	440g 15½oz		Cook 3 minutes, stirring once during cooking time. Leave to stand for 1 minute.	Cover
Tinned vegetables				
7½oz can Baked beans	215g 7½oz		Cook 1½ minutes, stirring once during cooking.	
15oz can Garden peas or other small vegetables	425g 15oz		Cook 4½ minutes, stirring 3 times during cooking.	
15½oz can Baked beans	440g 15½oz		Cook 2½ minutes, stirring once during cooking.	
Frozen cakes and bread				
Slice of home-made cake	Slice of home-made cake Slice of home-made cake	Heat ¾–1¼ minutes depending on size and type.		Stand on plate or paper.

Prawn stuffed tomatoes **A good starter—firm and attractive after six minutes in the microwave. (Recipe page 34)**

Food	Metric and American	Time to thaw	Time to cook	Comments
Frozen jam doughnuts	Frozen jam doughnuts Frozen jam doughnuts	Heat 1 minute for 1; 1½ minutes for 2.		Stand on plate or paper.
Frozen cream cake	Frozen cream cake Frozen cream cake	Heat 45 seconds. Leave to stand for 3 minutes.		Stand on plate or paper.
Melted cheese sandwich (2 slices of buttered toast with cheese.)	Melted cheese sandwich Melted cheese sandwich		30 seconds	Stand on plate.
Slice of frozen bread	Slice of frozen bread Slice of frozen bread	Heat ¾–1¼ minutes, depending on size and thickness of slice.		
Large loaf of bread, frozen	Large loaf of bread, frozen Large loaf of bread frozen	Heat 2 minutes. Leave to stand for 6 minutes. Heat further 2 minutes.		
½lb frozen butter	225g 1 cup	Heat 30 seconds. Leave to stand for 30 seconds. Heat further 15 seconds. Leave to stand for 30 seconds.		
Frozen plate meal (reheating)	Frozen plate meal Frozen plate meal	Heat 1 minute. Leave to stand for 5 minutes.	3 minutes	Cover.
Frozen individual meals (*'Boil-in-Bag'*) eg Braised kidneys in gravy	Braised kidneys in gravy Braised kidneys in gravy	Heat 2 minutes. Leave to stand for 2 minutes	1½ minutes	Slit bag crossways before cooking for ease of serving
Frozen individual chicken curry with uncooked rice	Frozen individual chicken curry with uncooked rice Frozen individual chicken curry with uncooked rice	Heat 2 minutes. Leave to stand for 5 minutes.	Cook 3 minutes. Bring salt water to boil, add rice. Cook 4 minutes. Leave to stand for 5 minutes. Cook further ½ minute.	

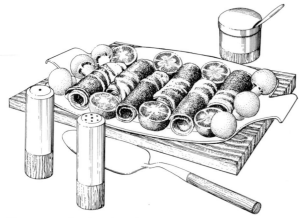

Hot cocoa (makes 1cup)

Measure out 175ml or just under 2dl (6 fluid oz or ¾ cup) cold milk. Place 3 x 5ml level teaspoons (3 level teaspoons or American 4½ level teaspoons) cocoa powder and same amount of sugar into large cup or mug. (No sugar or more sugar may be added according to taste.) Mix smoothly with a little of the cold milk then whisk in remainder. Heat in microwave about 2¼ minutes or until cocoa just comes up to the boil. Stir and serve.

Milky coffee

Make exactly as cocoa, substituting instant coffee to taste for the cocoa powder.

Leftover coffee

Leftover percolated or filtered ground coffee has no taste of staleness if reheated, in cups, for 1 or 2 minutes in the microwave.

Porridge

For 1 serving, place 2 x 15ml slightly rounded tablespoons (2 rounded tablespoons or American 3 rounded tablespoons) porridge into bowl. Add 150ml or 1½dl (¼pt or American ⅝ cup) water and a pinch of salt. Mix well. Cook, uncovered, 1¾ minutes in the microwave,

stirring twice. Leave to stand 1 or 2 minutes. Serve with milk or cream and sugar.

For 2 bowls: cook 3 to 3½ minutes; *for 3 bowls:* cook 3½ to 4 minutes; *for 4 bowls:* cook 4 to 4½ minutes.
Note: do not freeze.

Bacon rashers (strips or slices)

Bacon cooks extremely well in the microwave and there is less shrinkage than if treated in the conventional way. Many recipe books on microwave cooking advise arranging the bacon in a paper-lined dish before cooking, but I have found that the rashers stick to the paper. Therefore I always cook my bacon in an unlined dish but cover it with paper to prevent spluttering. It is easy enough to drain the bacon after cooking.

For 1 rasher: cook ¾ to 1 minute; *for 2 rashers:* cook 1½ to 1¾ minutes; *for 3 rashers:* cook 2 to 2¼ minutes; *for 4 rashers:* cook 2½ to 2¾ minutes; *for 5 rashers:* cook 3 to 3½ minutes; *for 6 rashers:* cook 4 to 4½ minutes.

If bacon has been refrigerated and the rashers have stuck together, loosen by standing on paper in the microwave and warming for about 30 seconds. You will find the rashers should then separate easily.

Cooked tomatoes (Serves 4)

Cut 4 washed and dried tomatoes in half horizontally. Stand in ring on a large plate, cut sides uppermost. Top with flakes of butter then sprinkle with salt and pepper to taste. Cook 3 to 4 minutes or until hot, turning plate twice. Serve straight away.

Note: do not freeze.

Whole cooked mushrooms (Serves 4 as a side dish)

Melt 25g (1 oz or American ⅛ cup) butter or margarine in the microwave. Add 125g (5oz or American about 1¼ cups) trimmed button mushrooms. Stir well in the butter. Cover dish. Cook in the microwave 2½ to 3 minutes or until hot. Serve straight away.

Sliced cooked mushrooms (Serves same number as above)

Follow above recipe but cook only 1½ to 2 minutes.

Note: do not freeze either of these dishes.

Baked beans on toast

Spread a freshly made slice of toast with butter or margarine. Stand on a plate. Top with 3 to 4 x 15ml heaped tablespoons (3 to 4 heaped tablespoons or American 4½ to 6 heaped tablespoons) baked beans. Heat, uncovered, 1½ to 2 minutes in the microwave.

For 2 plates: allow 2½ to 3½ minutes.

Canned spaghetti in tomato sauce on toast

Prepare exactly as baked beans on toast.

Canned spaghetti rings or alphabets in tomato sauce on toast

Prepare exactly as baked beans on toast.

Cheesy baked beans on toast

Prepare exactly as baked beans on toast but top with 1 or 2 slices processed cheese or 3 x 15ml rounded tablespoons (3 rounded tablespoons or American 4½ rounded tablespoons) grated Cheddar cheese. Heat about 1½ minutes, uncovered, in the microwave when the cheese should be melting and bubbling and the beans hot.

Welsh rarebit

Spread a freshly made slice of toast with butter or margarine. Stand on a plate. Top with 2 slices of processed cheese or 50g (2oz) grated Cheddar cheese. Heat, uncovered, in the microwave for ½ to ¾ minute or until cheese is melting and bubbling.

Buck rarebit

Make Welsh rarebit as above then top with a poached or fried egg (see Egg section).

Standby plate meals

Extremely useful to have available are plates of lunch or dinner consisting of meat, vegetables, gravy or sauce and trimmings. To prepare, place slices of cold cooked meat (such as beef, lamb, pork, veal, chicken, duck, turkey, ham, boiled bacon, sausages or hamburgers) on the centre of a dinner plate. Encircle with cooked vegetables, trying to keep the depth of the vegetables even all the way round. If appropriate, add trimmings such as bacon rolls, chipolata sausages, tomato halves, a few cooked mushrooms, bread sauce, etc. Make up as many plates as are required for a particular meal or meals. Cover each with cling film and deep freeze until required. To serve, make 2 slits in the film then reheat plates individually in the microwave until the ingredients are piping hot. Allow anything from 5 to 9 minutes, depending on contents of plate and type of cooker, and turn plate several times during cooking. It is not necessary to thaw the food before microwaving.

Note: avoid uneven mounds of vegetables, etc as this will result in uneven cooking. Similarly one type of food should not be piled on top of another.

Christmas pudding No longer an all-day job. Cook for four minutes, rest for five, then cook for a further two minutes. (Recipe page 95)

Christmas dinner

Plates of Christmas dinner—turkey, roast and boiled potatoes, sausages, bacon rolls, vegetables, cranberry and bread sauces together with gravy—can be prepared and cooked exactly as above. To save last-minute steaming of the pudding, make up Christmas pudding or puddings (see Pudding section) and, after turning out of basins and cooling, cut into serving size portions and stand on individual plates. Cover with cling film. Freeze. Slit film. Reheat from freezing until hot; about 1–2 minutes, depending on size of portion and type of cooker. Turn plate at least twice during cooking.

Eggs

A microwave is a perfect vehicle for cooking egg dishes. They neither stick, misbehave nor flop and a near-perfect omelet can be made in minutes, scrambled eggs in seconds and specialities, such as the French oeufs en cocotte, turn out like a chef's pièce de résistance. Provided times are carefully observed, yolks of fried and poached eggs remain creamy and soft, while the whites set gently without becoming chewy, tough and indigestible. The only thing you cannot do in a microwave is boil eggs—they simply explode! Similarly you will notice that recipes for fried, poached and baked egg dishes all have the yolks pierced with the tip of a pointed knife before cooking in order to puncture the surrounding skin and prevent a subsequent explosion.

Scrambled eggs

In a teacup, beat 1 x grade 3 (1 standard or American 1 medium) egg with 2 x 5ml teaspoons (2 teaspoons or American 3 teaspoons) milk. Add half the amount of butter. Beat egg mixture well and season to taste. Cook, uncovered, 30 seconds in microwave. Beat well. Cook further 10 to 15 seconds or until egg is only just set. Beat and serve.

For 2 eggs: double ingredients. Cook 45 seconds. Beat.

Cook further 20 to 30 seconds. Beat. *For 3 eggs:* treble ingredients. Cook 1 minute. Beat. Cook further 35 to 50 seconds. Beat. *For 4 eggs:* quadruple ingredients. Cook $1\frac{1}{2}$ minutes. Beat. Cook further minute, beating twice.

Notes: do not overcook as eggs will become rubbery. Do not freeze.

Poached eggs

Pour 6 tablespoons hot water and $\frac{1}{4}$ x 5ml teaspoon ($\frac{1}{4}$ teaspoon or American $\frac{1}{2}$ teaspoon) mild vinegar into shallow dish. Bring to boil in the microwave; about $1\frac{1}{2}$ minutes. Carefully break 1 egg into dish. Puncture yolk in two places with tip of a pointed knife. Stand dish in microwave and cover with a plate. (Avoid paper as it could fall into dish.) Cook 45 seconds to $1\frac{1}{4}$ minutes depending on how well cooked you like the white. Leave to stand 1 minute. Remove from dish with slotted fish slice.

For 2 eggs: cook 1 to $1\frac{1}{2}$ minutes; *for 3 eggs:* cook $1\frac{1}{2}$ to $2\frac{1}{2}$ minutes.

Note: remember to cook eggs in individual dishes, ie one egg per dish, so if you are cooking 3 eggs at a time, you should be using 3 small dishes.

Fried eggs

For a 1-egg serving, melt 1 x 5ml heaped teaspoon (1 heaped teaspoon or American $1\frac{1}{2}$ heaped teaspoons) butter in a small dish for 30 seconds in the microwave. Gently break in egg. Pierce yolk twice with a pointed knife. Cover dish with plate. Cook 30 seconds. Leave to stand 1 minute. Uncover. Cook further 15 seconds when white should be just set; if not, allow an extra 10 to 15 seconds.

For 2 fried eggs in a dish, cook 1 minute and 5 seconds. Leave to stand 1 minute. Uncover. Cook further 15 to 30 seconds.

Notes: It is not advisable to cook more than 2 eggs at a time in the same dish as there is the danger that the extra long cooking time needed to set the whites will toughen the yolks.
Do not freeze.

Oeufs en cocotte (Serves 1)

Ingredients	Imperial	American
15g butter	½oz	1 tbsp
2 x grade 3 eggs	2 standard	2 medium
1 x 15ml tbsp whipping cream	1 tbsp	1½ tbsp
2 x 5ml level tsp chopped chives or parsley	2 level tsp	3 level tsp
salt and pepper to taste	to taste	to taste

1 Stand butter in fairly small glass or pottery dish. Melt ½ minute in microwave.
2 Carefully break in eggs. Pierce yolks in two places with tip of a pointed knife.
3 Coat with cream then sprinkle with chives or parsley and salt and pepper.
4 Place in microwave. Cover with plate. Cook 1 minute. Leave to stand, covered, a further minute.
5 Serve with crusty rolls and butter.

Note: do not freeze.

American omelet (Serves 1 generously)

Ingredients	Imperial	American
15g butter	½oz	1 tbsp
3 x grade 3 eggs	3 standard	3 medium
2 x 15ml tbsp milk	2 tbsp	3 tbsp
½ x 5ml level tsp salt	½ level tsp	¾ level tsp
pepper to taste	to taste	to taste

1 Melt butter for ½ minute in a 20cm (8in) shallow glass pie dish with straight sides. Remove from oven. Brush butter evenly over base.
2 Beat together rest of ingredients. Pour into dish. Place in microwave. Cover with a plate.
3 Cook 1½ minutes. Uncover. Stir eggs gently, bringing edges towards centre. Cover. Cook a further 1½ minutes.
4 Uncover. Cook further ½ to 1 minute, according to whether you like an omelet still slightly moist or more on the dryish side. Fold into three and slide out on to a plate.

French omelet

Make exactly as above, substituting water for milk.

Cheese omelet

Make either omelet as directed. Sprinkle with 2 x 15ml heaped tablespoons (2 heaped tablespoons or American 3 tablespoons) finely grated Cheddar or Edam cheese before folding.

Mushroom omelet

Make either omelet as directed. Sprinkle with 2 x 15ml heaped tablespoons (2 heaped tablespoons or American 3 tablespoons) thinly sliced and butter-fried mushrooms before folding.

Ham omelet

Make either omelet as directed. Sprinkle with 2 x 15ml heaped tablespoons (2 heaped tablespoons or American 3 tablespoons) finely chopped ham before folding.

Tomato omelet

Make either omelet as directed. Cover with 2 medium sized, skinned, chopped and butter-fried tomatoes before folding.

Omelet aux fines herbes

Add the following to either of the beaten egg mixtures before cooking: 2 x 15ml level teaspoons (2 level teaspoons or American 3 level teaspoons) each of chopped parsley, chopped chives and chopped mint. If fresh herbs are unavailable, substitute ⅓ of the quantity mixed dried herbs. Cook and fold as directed.

Note: do not freeze any of the above omelets.

Spanish omelet (Serves 2 generously)

Ingredients	Imperial	American
25g butter	1oz	⅛ cup
2 x 5ml tsp olive oil	2 tsp	3 tsp
125g skinned tomatoes, chopped	4oz	2 medium
125g cooked potatoes, diced	4oz	¾ cup
125g onion, finely chopped	4oz	1 large
50g green pepper, finely chopped	2oz	1 small or ½ medium
4 x grade 3 eggs	4 standard	4 medium
4 x 5ml tsp water	4 tsp	6 tsp
1 x 5ml level tsp salt	1 level tsp	1½ level tsp

1   Place butter in 20cm (8in) pie plate of at least 2½cm (1in) in depth. Melt 1 minute in microwave. Add oil and vegetables. Cook, uncovered, 4 minutes. Stir twice.

2   Beat eggs with water and salt. Pour into dish over vegetables. Cook, uncovered, 1 minute. Stir well, bringing edges of cooked eggs towards centre. Cook further minute. Stir well. Cook, uncovered, 1 minute. Stand 1 minute. Cut into 2 portions and serve hot.

Notes: Spanish omelets are never folded.
Do not freeze.

Traditional Swiss fondue (Serves 4)

Ingredients	Imperial	American
1 large garlic clove	1 large	1 large
200g grated Emmental cheese	7oz	just over 1½ cups
400g grated Gruyère cheese	14oz	about 3⅓ cups
4 x 5ml level tsp cornflour	4 level tsp	6 level tsp cornstarch
275ml or 3dl dry white Swiss or French wine	½pt	1¼ cups
1 x 5ml tsp lemon juice	1 tsp	1½ tsp
1 x 15ml tbsp Kirsch	1 tbsp	1½ tbsp
black pepper to taste	to taste	to taste

1   Halve garlic clove and press against sides of a handled pottery dish or a traditional Swiss fondue pot called a 'Caquelon'. For a stronger flavour, crush the garlic directly into the pot.

2   Stir in next five ingredients. Cook, uncovered, in the microwave for 7 to 8 minutes or until fondue comes to boil and begins to bubble. Stir at least twice.

3   Remove from oven and gently whisk in Kirsch. Season with pepper. Stand dish over a spirit stove on the table so that the fondue keeps hot. Provide a bowl of diced up French bread and long-handled forks.

4   To eat, spear bread on forks and stir round in fondue mixture. Lift out and eat straight away.

5   The recommended drinks to accompany a fondue are cups of hot lemon tea and small glasses of ice-cold Kirsch. Long, chilled drinks should be avoided.

Notes: do not freeze.
If liked, add a few pinches of grated nutmeg with the cornflour.

2 Starters

The recipes in this section represent a short selection of hot and appetising starters with plenty of variety. Macaroni alla carbonara and pâtés apart, all can be made while guests are enjoying a pre-meal drink.

Party ham pâté (Serves 12)

Ingredients	Imperial	American
¾kg lean ham	1½lb	3 cups closely packed
225g onion	8oz	1 large
25g parsley	1oz	1oz
4 x grade 3 eggs	4 standard	4 medium
1 x 5ml level tsp dried sage	1 level tsp	1½ level tsp
pepper to taste	to taste	to taste

1   Using cling film, line a round, straight-sided glass or pottery dish of 18¾cm (7½in) in diameter. The depth should be about 7½cm (3in).

2   Very finely mince or grind ham until it takes on a paste-like appearance. Repeat with peeled onion and parsley.

3   Place ham, onion, parsley, eggs, sage and pepper into a large bowl. Beat until absolutely smooth.

4   Spoon evenly into prepared dish. Cover with cling film, making 2 slits in it with scissors to prevent it 'ballooning-up' in oven.

5   Cook 10 minutes. Rest 5 minutes. Half turn dish. Cook 5 minutes. Half turn dish. Rest 10 minutes. Cook 5 minutes.

6   Remove from microwave and leave until completely cold before cutting into twelve portions. Accompany with salad and hot buttered toast.

Notes: this is a moist and flavourful pâté which, as no breadcrumbs have been included, will particularly appeal to slimmers. For added piquancy, 1 or 2 peeled garlic cloves may be minced with the onion.

You will notice that as the pâté cooks, it browns round the edges. This browning has no adverse effect on either the flavour or the texture.

Do not freeze.

Party ham pate   Stays moist and full of flavour; an excellent recipe for slimmers. (Receipe page 31)

Cheese and mushroom pie **Like a quiche lorraine, but use mushrooms instead of bacon.** **(Recipe page 120)**

Liver pâté (Serves 8 to 10)

Ingredients	Imperial	American
1 x 15ml tbsp corn oil	1 tbsp	1½ tbsp
½kg lamb's liver (without tubes and gristle)	1lb	16oz
50g pork fat, chopped	2oz	2oz
50g onion, chopped	2oz	1 small
125g pork sausagemeat	4oz	4oz
6 x 15ml level tbsp fresh white breadcrumbs	6 level tbsp	9 level tbsp
2 egg yolks	2	2
2½ x 15 ml tbsp brandy	2½ tbsp	3¾ tbsp
¼ to ½ x 15ml level tsp black pepper	¼ to ½ level tsp	½ to ¾ level tsp
6 streaky bacon rashers (strips)	6	6
Garnish		
sliced gherkins to taste	to taste	to taste
sliced tomatoes to taste	to taste	to taste

1 Pour oil into fairly shallow glass or pottery dish. Heat, uncovered, 2 minutes in the microwave.
2 Add liver, cut into thin pieces. Toss in oil. Cook, uncovered, 2 minutes. Add pork fat. Heat a further minute. Add onion to mixture then mince all cooked ingredients.
3 Combine with sausagemeat, crumbs, yolks, brandy and pepper. Stir thoroughly to mix.
4 Brush a 1½l (3pt) glass or pottery dish with melted butter or oil. Line with de-rinded bacon. Place pâté mixture into dish over bacon. Spread evenly with a knife. Cover dish with cling film. Make 2 slits in it with scissors to prevent it from 'ballooning-up' in oven.
5 Cook 12 minutes, giving dish a quarter turn at the end of every 3 minutes. Cool for 10 minutes. To press, place weights on a saucer over the pâté. Refrigerate overnight.
6 Next day, turn out on to a platter and garnish with gherkins and tomatoes. Cut into slices and serve with toast.

Note: do not freeze.

Mushroom vol-au-vents (Serves 6)

Ingredients	Imperial	American
25g butter	1oz	⅛ cup
25g flour	1oz	¼ cup
275ml or 3dl milk	½pt	1¼ cups
1 x 5ml level tsp Continental mustard	1 level tsp	1½ level tsp
225g canned mushrooms in brine	8oz	1 cup
salt and pepper to taste	to taste	to taste
6 large vol-au-vent cases, *already baked*, each 7½ x 3¾cm	3 x 1½in	3 x 1½in

1 To make sauce, melt butter for 1 minute in deepish glass or pottery dish. Stir in flour. Gradually whisk in milk.
2 Cook a total of 5 minutes, whisking sauce every minute to prevent lumps from forming. Remove from oven and whisk in mustard. Add drained and halved mushrooms then season to taste with salt and pepper.
3 Spoon equal amounts of mushroom mixture into vol-au-vent cases. Add pastry lids (usually found inside the cases if shop bought), then stand in a ring on a dinner plate.
4 Cook 4 minutes, half turning plate after 2 minutes. Serve straight away.

Chicken vol-au-vents

Substitute 125g (4oz or American ¾ cup) diced cooked chicken for mushrooms. Omit mustard and flavour sauce with finely grated peel of ½ medium lemon. Season.

Prawn vol-au-vents

Substitute 125g (4 oz or American ¾ cup) peeled prawns for mushrooms. Flavour sauce with mustard, a squeeze of fresh lemon juice and a little finely chopped parsley. Season.

Prawn stuffed tomatoes (Serves 6)

Ingredients	Imperial	American
6 medium tomatoes	6 medium	6 medium
50g fresh white breadcrumbs	2oz	1 cup (loosely packed)
1 x 5ml tsp dried basil	1 level tsp	1½ level tsp
½ x 5ml tsp onion salt	½ level tsp	¾ level tsp
2 x 5ml tsp salad oil	2 tsp	2½ tsp
2 x 5ml tsp Worcester sauce	2 tsp	2½ tsp
salt and pepper to taste	to taste	to taste
75g peeled prawns	3oz	½ cup
parsley sprigs for garnishing	for garnishing	for garnishing

1 Cut tops off tomatoes. Cut a thin sliver off the base of each tomato so that it stands upright without toppling.
2 Using teaspoon, carefully scoop pulp into bowl. Discard hard and woody cores. Stand tomatoes upside down to drain on kitchen paper.
3 Add all remaining ingredients to tomato pulp, reserving one third of the prawns for garnishing. Mix thoroughly using a fork.
4 Pile stuffing into tomatoes then top each with a prawn and small sprig of parsley. Arrange in a ring on a plate and cook for 6 minutes.

Note: do not freeze.

Mushroom and onion stuffed tomatoes (Serves 6)

Ingredients	Imperial	American
6 medium tomatoes	6 medium	6 medium
25g butter	1oz	⅛ cup
1 medium chopped onion	1 medium	1 medium
1 medium garlic clove, crushed	1 medium	1 medium
4 medium trimmed mushrooms, chopped	4 medium	4 medium
4 x 15ml tbsp fresh white breadcrumbs	4 level tbsp	6 level tbsp
salt and pepper to taste	to taste	to taste
2 x 15ml tbsp grated Parmesan cheese	2 level tbsp	2½ level tbsp

1 Cut tops off tomatoes and keep on one side for lids. Cut a thin sliver off the base of each tomato so that it stands upright without toppling.
2 Using a teaspoon, carefully scoop pulp into bowl. Discard hard and woody cores. Stand tomatoes upside down to drain on kitchen paper.
3 Place butter in shallow dish and melt, uncovered, for 1 minute. Add onion and garlic. Stir round in butter. Cook, uncovered, 2 minutes. Add mushrooms and stir round. Cook, uncovered, a further 2 minutes.
4 Remove dish from oven. Stir in tomato pulp and crumbs. Season to taste. Spoon into tomatoes. Replace lids at a slight angle then sprinkle with cheese.
5 Arrange in a ring on a plate and cook for 6 minutes. Serve on rounds of fried bread.

Note: do not freeze.

Romanian style 'braised' mushrooms (Serves 4)

Ingredients	Imperial	American
½kg mushrooms	1lb	about 5 cups
50g butter	2oz	¼ cup
2 medium garlic cloves	2 medium	2 medium
2 x 15ml rounded tbsp chopped parsley	2 rounded tbsp	3 rounded tbsp
1 x 15ml tbsp lemon juice	1 tbsp	1½ tbsp
½ to 1 x 5ml level tsp salt	1 level tsp	1½ level tsp

1 Wash, trim and dry mushrooms. Peel if skins are discoloured. Slice very thinly.
2 Place butter and crushed garlic into a deepish glass or pottery dish. Heat 3 minutes in microwave.
3 Add mushrooms. Stir so that all the slices are well-coated with butter, etc. Cook, uncovered, 2 minutes. Remove from oven. Stir well. Cook, uncovered, a further minute.
4 Remove from microwave. Stir in parsley, lemon juice and salt. Pile on to 4 plates. Serve hot with crusty brown rolls and butter.

Note: do not freeze.

Mock caviar blinis (Serves 6)

Ingredients	Imperial	American
6 cooked pancakes each 20cm	8in	8in
100g lumpfish caviar	3½oz	about ½ cup
150ml or 1½dl soured cream	¼pt	⅝ cup
50g butter	2oz	¼ cup
2 x 5ml tsp lemon juice	2 tsp	2 tsp

1 Spread pancakes out on work surface. Combine caviar and soured cream well together.
2 Spoon equal amounts on to pancakes then fold up into parcels by bringing edges over centres.
3 Place butter in large but not too deep glass or pottery dish. Melt 2 minutes in microwave. Add pancakes, with folds underneath. Baste with melted butter. Moisten with lemon juice.
4 Cook, uncovered, 5 minutes in microwave. Half turn dish after 2½ minutes. Serve hot, accompanied by wedges of lemon.

Note: do not freeze.

Crab toasts (Serves 4)

Ingredients	Imperial	American
4 large slices freshly made toast	4 large slices	4 large slices
About 40g butter	1½oz	3 tbsp
225g fresh or frozen crabmeat	8oz	1 cup
1 x 15ml rounded tbsp chopped parsley	1 rounded tbsp	1½ rounded tbsp
175g grated Cheddar or Edam cheese	6oz	1½ cups

1 Butter toast. Spread each piece with equal amounts of crabmeat. Sprinkle with parsley, followed by cheese.
2 Stand on individual plates. Cook, one at a time, in the microwave for 1¼ to 1½ minutes or until cheese is melting and bubbly. Serve straight away.

Note: do not freeze.

Macaroni alla carbonara (Serves 4 to 6)

Ingredients	Imperial	American
25g butter	1oz	⅛ cup
50g bacon	2oz	2 strips
225g elbow or broken macaroni	8oz	2 cups
575ml or 6dl boiling water	1pt	2½ cups
3 x 15ml tbsp double cream	3 tbsp	4½ tbsp
2 x grade 3 eggs	2 standard	2 medium
3 x 15ml level tbsp grated Parmesan cheese	3 level tbsp	4½ level tbsp

1 Place butter in large glass or pottery dish. Melt 1 minute in microwave. Add finely chopped bacon. Stir round. Cook, uncovered, 2 minutes.

2 Stir in macaroni and water. Cook, uncovered, 12 minutes, giving dish a quarter turn every 3 minutes. Cover. Leave to stand 10 to 15 minutes or until macaroni has swollen and absorbed all the water.
3 Beat rest of ingredients well together. Add to macaroni. Toss with 2 spoons. You will find that the heat of the pasta partially cooks the egg mixture as you are tossing. Return to microwave. Cook, uncovered, 2 minutes.
4 Adjust seasoning to taste, pile on to plates and serve hot. If liked, pass extra grated Parmesan cheese separately.

Note: do not freeze.

Baked salmon stuffed avocados (Serves 4)

Ingredients	Imperial	American
1 x 100g small can red salmon	3oz	½ cup
50g onion	2oz	1 small
50g fresh white breadcrumbs	2oz	1 cup
2 medium ripe avocados	2 medium	2 medium
1 x 15ml tbsp lemon juice	1 tbsp	1½ tbsp
½ x 5ml level tsp salt	½ level tsp	¾ level tsp
4 x 5ml level tsp salted peanuts	4 level tsp	6 level tsp
paprika for sprinkling	for sprinkling	for sprinkling

1 Tip salmon and liquor from can into bowl. Mash well. Very finely grate peeled onion. Add to salmon with crumbs.
2 Halve avocados. Scoop flesh into bowl with teaspoon, leaving 1¼cm (½in) thick avocado shells. Add

Trout with almonds 50g or 2oz of almonds transforms a simple-looking dish into a luxurious one. (Receipe page 43)

lemon juice. Mash flesh with stainless fork. Add to salmon mixture. Mix thoroughly. Season with salt.

3 Pile mixture into avocado shells. Sprinkle with peanuts and paprika. Arrange around the outside of a large plate.

4 Cook, uncovered, a total of 8 minutes, giving plate a quarter turn every 2 minutes. Serve hot with crisp toast.

Note: do not freeze.

Tuna and artichoke au gratin (Serves 6)

Ingredients	Imperial	American
15g butter	½oz	1 tbsp
75g bacon	3oz	3 strips
198g canned tuna	7oz	just under 1 cup
400g undrained weight canned artichoke hearts	14oz un-drained weight	about 1¾ cups
125g cooked, diced potato	4oz	1 cup
150ml or 1½dl soured cream	¼ pint	⅝ cup

Topping

1 x 15ml level tbsp lightly toasted breadcrumbs	1 level tbsp	1½ level tbsp
3 x 5ml level tsp grated Parmesan cheese	3 level tsp	4½ level tsp
15g butter	½oz	1 tbsp
paprika for sprinkling	for sprinkling	for sprinkling

1 Place butter in medium-sized glass or pottery dish. Melt ½ minute. Chop bacon finely. Add to butter. Stir well. Cook, uncovered, 1 minute.

2 Drain tuna and mash finely. Combine with butter and bacon in dish. Drain artichoke hearts and cut into quarters. Stand on top of tuna with diced potatoes.

3 Beat cream until smooth, adding 1 x 15ml table-spoon milk (1 tablespoon or American 1½ tablespoons) if cream is on the thick side. Pour over tuna and potatoes.

4 Sprinkle with crumbs and Parmesan cheese then top with flakes of butter. Dust lightly with paprika. Cook, uncovered, 6 minutes. Half turn dish after 3 minutes. Serve with freshly made toast.

Note: this dish is suitable for freezing.

3 Soups

Home-made soups—for winter and summer eating—are always welcome and I have included a few popular 'brews' as well as instructions for dealing with condensed and packet soups. Ready-to-serve canned or home-made soups should be poured into a jug or individual plates, covered and then heated for a few minutes in the microwave.

Clear chicken soup (Serves 6)

Ingredients	Imperial	American
¾kg chicken pieces to include giblets, wings, etc	1½lb	24oz
250g onions	8oz	2 large
175g carrots	6oz	2 medium
1 bouquet garni	1	1
1¼l or 12dl boiling water	2pt	5 cups
2 x 5ml level tsp salt	2 level tsp	3 level tsp

1   Place chicken pieces, in single layer, in deepish glass or pottery dish. Cover with lid or cling film. (If using film, make 2 slits in it with scissors to prevent it from 'ballooning-up' in oven.) Cook ¼ hour, half turning dish after 7½ minutes.
2   Thinly slice carrots and onions. Add to dish of chicken with bouquet garni, water and salt. Cover (making slits in film as before). Cook ½ hour, half turning dish after 15 minutes.
3   Leave soup until lukewarm. Strain liquid. As it is fairly concentrated, add an extra 275ml or 3dl (½pt or 1¼ American cups) hot water and adjust seasoning.
4   Pour into clean dish. Cover. Reheat in microwave 4 to 5 minutes or until boiling. Serve with vermicelli or cooked rice.

Easy chicken broth (Serves 6)

Place cooked vegetables from above soup in large and clean dish. Cut up edible pieces of chicken and add. Stir in 3 x 15ml level tablespoons rolled oats (3 level tablespoons or American 4½ level tablespoons), ¾l or 9dl boiling water (1½pt or 3¾ American cups), 2 x 5ml level teaspoons salt (2 level teaspoons or American 4 level teaspoons) and 2 x 15ml level tablespoons (2 level tablespoons or American 3 level tablespoons) finely chopped parsley. Stir well to mix. Cover. Cook $\frac{1}{4}$ hour, half turning dish after $7\frac{1}{2}$ minutes.

French onion soup (Serves 6)

Ingredients	Imperial	American
50g butter	2oz	$\frac{1}{4}$ cup
$\frac{1}{2}$kg onions	1lb	1lb
4 x 5ml level tsp cornflour	4 level tsp	5 level tsp cornstarch
1 brown gravy cube	1	1
$\frac{3}{4}$l boiling beef stock	$1\frac{1}{2}$pt	$3\frac{3}{4}$ cups bouillon
6 slices French bread each $2\frac{1}{2}$cm thick	each 1in thick	each 1in thick
6 x 15ml heaped tbsp grated Cheddar cheese	6 heaped tbsp	9 heaped tbsp

1 Heat butter for 2 minutes in large and deep glass or pottery dish. Add onions. Cook, uncovered, 5 minutes.
2 Stir in cornflour then crumble in stock cube. Gradually blend in stock, stirring well.
3 Cover dish with cling film, making 2 slits in it with scissors to prevent it from 'ballooning-up' in oven.
4 Cook $\frac{1}{2}$ hour, turning dish 4 times. Stand 5 minutes.
5 Uncover. Stir soup well. Ladle into 6 soup bowls. Top each with a slice of bread.
6 Sprinkle bread with cheese. Return each bowl to microwave for 1 to $1\frac{1}{2}$ minutes or until cheese melts. Serve straight away.

Note: do not freeze.

Cream of carrot soup (Serves 4 to 6)

Ingredients	Imperial	American
350g carrots	12oz	12oz
125g onion	4oz	4oz
25g butter	1oz	$\frac{1}{8}$ cup
2 x 15ml tbsp water	2 tbsp	3 tbsp
425ml or 4dl milk	$\frac{3}{4}$pt	$1\frac{1}{2}$ cups
1 x 15ml level tbsp cornflour	1 level tbsp	$1\frac{1}{2}$ level tbsp cornstarch
150ml or $1\frac{1}{2}$dl water	$\frac{1}{4}$pt	$\frac{5}{8}$ cup
1 x 5ml level tsp salt	1 level tsp	$1\frac{1}{2}$ level tsp

1 Very thinly slice carrots and onions. Place in deep-ish glass or pottery dish with butter and the table-spoons of water. Cover. Cook 12 minutes in the micro-wave, stirring twice.
2 Transfer ingredients to liquidiser goblet. Add milk. Blend until smooth.
3 Return to dish. Add cornflour mixed to smooth cream with water. Season with salt. Cook, uncovered, in the microwave for 6 minutes, stirring briskly at the end of every minute.
4 Adjust seasoning to taste. Pour into soup bowls or cups and sprinkle with chopped chives, parsley or mint.

Note: this soup is suitable for freezing.

Cream of vegetable soup

Instead of carrots, use same amount of either cauli-flower florets, diced parsnips, diced swedes or diced marrow. Keep quantity of onion the same.

Green pea soup (Serves 6)

Ingredients	Imperial	American
$\frac{1}{2}$kg frozen peas	1lb	4 cups
4 x 15ml tbsp hot water	4 tbsp	6 tbsp
425ml or 4dl cold water	$\frac{3}{4}$pt	$1\frac{1}{2}$ cups
1 chicken stock cube	1	1
1 x 15ml level tbsp cornflour	1 level tbsp	$1\frac{1}{2}$ level tbsp cornstarch
1 x 15ml level tsp salt	1 level tsp	$1\frac{1}{2}$ level tsp
275ml or 3dl milk	$\frac{1}{2}$pt	$1\frac{1}{4}$ cups
6 x 15ml tbsp single (or coffee) cream	6 tbsp	9 tbsp
curry powder for sprinkling	for sprinkling	for sprinkling

1 Place frozen peas in deep dish with the tablespoons of hot water. Cover. Cook 8 minutes.
2 Place in blender goblet. Add all remaining ingredients except milk, cream and curry powder. Blend until smooth. Return to washed and dried dish.
3 Stir in milk, cover and cook 6-8 minutes or until boiling. Ladle into warm tureen, swirl in cream then sprinkle with curry powder.

Note: if preferred, paprika may be used instead of curry powder.

Minestrone soup Substantial for a cold day—and a
home-made soup is always welcome. (Recipe page 41)

Soups **41**

Minestrone (Serves 8 to 10)

Ingredients	Imperial	American
350g marrow, diced	12oz	about 4 cups
225g carrots, diced	8oz	about 3 cups
225g potatoes, diced	8oz	about 3 cups
225g onion, finely chopped	8oz	about 3 cups
225g cabbage, finely shredded	8oz	about 2½ cups
125g whole frozen green beans	4oz	4oz
396g canned tomatoes	14oz	1¾ cups
50g macaroni	2oz	½ cup
1¼l or 12dl boiling water	2pt	5 cups
1 x 5ml level tsp salt	1 level tsp	1½ level tsp
3 x 15ml heaped tbsp baked beans in tomato sauce	3 heaped tbsp	4½ heaped tbsp —
2 x 15ml level tbsp tomato purée	2 level tbsp	3 level tbsp

1   Place all prepared vegetables into large bowl. Add tomatoes and macaroni. Cover. Cook 10 minutes. Stir well. Add ¾l (1½pt) water. Cover. Cook 24 minutes, giving dish a quarter turn at the end of every 6 minutes.
2   Stand 10 minutes. Uncover. Stir in rest of water and all remaining ingredients. Stir well to mix, breaking up canned tomatoes with a fork. Serve hot and pass grated Parmesan cheese separately.

Note: this soup is suitable for freezing.

Chilled cucumber and yogurt soup (Serves 6 to 8)

Ingredients	Imperial	American
25g butter	1oz	⅛ cup
1 large garlic clove	1 large	1 large
225g peeled and coarsely grated cucumber	8oz	1½ cups
575ml or 6dl natural yogurt	1pt	2½ cups
275ml or 3dl milk	½pt	1¼ cups
150ml or 1½dl cold water	¼pt	⅝ cup
1 x 5ml level tsp salt	1 level tsp	1½ level tsp
6 to 8 x 5ml tsp chopped mint	6 to 8 tsp	9 to 12 tsp

1   Place butter in deep glass or pottery dish. Melt 1 minute in microwave. Add crushed garlic and cucumber. Cook, uncovered, 4 minutes. Half turn dish after 2 minutes and stir contents.
2   Remove from oven. Whisk in yogurt, milk, water and salt. Chill, covered, in the refrigerator at least 4 hours.

3   Before serving, stir soup round and ladle into soup cups or bowls. Add an ice cube to each cup and sprinkle with mint.

Note: do not freeze.

Dehydrated soup mixes

Shower soup mix into a 1¼l (2pt) fairly deep glass or pottery dish. Gradually stir in cold water, using amount recommended on the packet. Leave to stand 20 minutes to give vegetables, etc time to soften. Stir. Cover. Cook 6 to 8 minutes in the microwave or until soup comes to the boil. Stir twice. Leave to stand 5 minutes. Stir and serve.

Canned condensed soup (275g or 10oz size)

Spoon soup into a jug such as a Pyrex Juggler. Add 1 can of boiling water. Whisk thoroughly. Put lid onto jug. Heat 6 to 7 minutes or until soup just comes up to boil. Whisk well 2 or 3 times during cooking. Pour into dishes and serve straight away.

Although some books suggest dividing soup out into individual bowls, adding water and whisking while cooking, I find it difficult to whisk the soup in a small bowl without making a mess and the jug method is far less awkward. Any leftovers can be kept in the jug and reheated in the microwave as needed.

4 Fish

Fish and a microwave were made for each other. Fish has always been on its best behaviour when poached quickly in a minimum of liquid; the very technique one uses in a microwave oven. Whether using fresh or frozen fish, the taste is impeccable and the texture of the flesh is creamy and tender. Please check the charts on defrosting and cooking frozen fish before you begin.

Fish defrosting and cooking guide

Fish which are normally steamed, baked or poached cook perfectly in the microwave oven. I would not recommend microwaving fish which has been coated with batter or breadcrumbs.

Points to remember:

1   To enhance flavour and appearance, brush fillets with butter and sprinkle with seasoning and herbs or paprika.

2   Always cook in a covered container.

3   Test fish at regular intervals during cooking. When it is cooked it will flake. Overcooking will cause toughness.

4   Do not deep fat fry in the microwave oven.

Fish	Weight	Time to thaw	Time to cook
Coley Plaice (American flounder) Haddock Cod, Salmon, Halibut, etc	500g (1lb) prepared fillets, cutlets or steaks	4–5 minutes	8–10 minutes
Smoked haddock, Smoked cod, etc	500g (1lb) prepared fillets, cutlets or steaks	4–5 minutes	6–8 minutes
Kippers	500g (1lb) fillets	2–3 minutes	3–4 minutes
Mackerel Herrings Trout	500g (1lb) gutted	2–3 minutes	5–6 minutes

Note: 'Boil-in-the-Bag' fish should have the bag pierced before cooking.

Lemon-soused herrings (Serves 4)

Ingredients	Imperial	American
4 herrings each 225g	each 8oz	medium
¼ x 5ml level tsp salt	¼ level tsp	½ level tsp
1 blade mace	1 blade	1 blade
1 medium bay leaf	1 medium	1 medium
6 peppercorns	6	6
2 cloves	2	2
150ml or 1½dl bottled lemon juice	¼pt	⅝ cup
150ml or 1½dl water	¼pt	⅝ cup
75g onion, sliced or chopped	3oz	1 medium

1 Clean and bone herrings, completely removing heads. (Alternatively, ask your fishmonger to do this for you.) Roll up, skin side outside, from head end to tail. Arrange in deepish glass or pottery dish.
2 Sprinkle with salt then add mace, bay leaf, peppercorns and cloves. Pour lemon juice and water into dish over herrings. Add onion.
3 Cover dish with lid or cling film. (If using film, make 2 slits in it with scissors to prevent it from 'ballooning-up' in oven.)
4 Cook in the microwave 6 minutes, half turning dish after 3 minutes. Leave herrings to cool in the cooking liquor then chill lightly in the refrigerator before serving.

Note: this dish is suitable for deep freezing.

Buttered plaice (Serves 2)

Ingredients	Imperial	American
40g butter	1½oz	3 tbsp
2 plaice, cleaned, each 225g	8oz	medium
salt and white pepper to taste	to taste	to taste

1 Melt butter 1½ minutes in large but shallow glass or pottery dish. Add cleaned plaice.
2 Turn over so that both sides are butter-coated. Sprinkle to taste with salt and white pepper.
3 Cover with lid or cling film. (If using film, make 2 slits with scissors to prevent it from 'ballooning-up' in oven.)
4 Cook 5 minutes, half turning dish after 2½ minutes.

Leave to rest 2 minutes. Uncover. Serve coated with juices from dish and vegetables to taste.

Buttered sole (Serves 2)

Follow above recipe but substitute 2 skinned soles (same weight and size) for plaice.

Note: do not freeze either of these dishes.

Trout with almonds (Serves 4)

Ingredients	Imperial	American
50g butter	2oz	¼ cup
50g split and toasted almonds	2oz	½ cup
4 trout, cleaned, each 175g	6oz	medium

1 Melt butter for 1½ minutes in a large but shallow oblong dish. Add almonds. Stir with butter. Cook, uncovered, 2 minutes.
2 Stand trout, side by side, in dish. Turn over so that both sides are butter-coated.
3 Cover with lid or cling film. (If using film, make 2 slits in it with scissors to prevent it from 'ballooning-up' in oven.)
4 Cook 5 minutes. Half turn dish. Cook further 4 minutes. Rest 3 minutes. Uncover dish and transfer fish to 4 warm dinner plates.
5 Coat with juices from dish and the almonds. Garnish with lemon wedges and parsley. Accompany with vegetables to taste.

Note: do not freeze.

Haddock with orange nut rice (Serves 4)

Ingredients	Imperial	American
50g butter	2oz	¼ cup
250g long grain rice ('Easy cook')	8oz	1⅓ cup
50g walnuts, chopped	2oz	½ cup
finely grated peel of 1 medium orange	1 medium	1 medium
550ml or 6dl water	1pt	2½ cups
2 x 5ml level tsp salt	2 level tsp	3 level tsp
skinned fresh haddock fillet (4 pieces), each 175g	each 6oz	each 6oz
1 small onion, peeled	1 small	1 small
sweet paprika for sprinkling	for sprinkling	for sprinkling

Lemon-soused herrings Any fish normally steamed, baked or poached cooks perfectly in a microwave, flavour and texture being retained at their best. (Recipe page 43)

1 Place half the butter in a large but fairly shallow dish. Melt, uncovered, 1 minute.

2 Add rice, walnuts, orange peel, water and salt. Cover with lid or cling film. (If using film, make 2 slits in it with scissors to prevent it from 'ballooning-up' in oven.) Cook ¼ hour, half turning dish after 7½ minutes.

3 Uncover. Arrange fish on top of rice. Cut onion into very thin slices then separate slices into rings. Place on fish. Sprinkle with paprika then dot with flakes of remaining butter.

4 Cover dish with lid or film (making slits in film as before). Cook 8 minutes, half turning dish after 4 minutes.

5 Leave to stand 3 minutes then serve fish and rice with a crisp green salad.

Note: this dish can be deep frozen for up to about 2 months.

Poached salmon steaks (Serves 4)

Ingredients	Imperial	American
4 salmon steaks,		
each 2½cm thick	each 1in thick	each 1in thick
8 x 15ml tbsp boiling water	8 tbsp	12 tbsp
1 x 15ml tbsp fresh lemon juice	1 tbsp	1½ tbsp
1 x 5ml level tsp salt	1 level tsp	1½ level tsp

1 Place salmon steaks (thaw frozen ones first) in large and shallow glass or pottery dish.

2 Pour water and lemon juice over fish. Sprinkle with salt. Cover dish with cling film, making 2 slits in it with scissors to prevent it from 'ballooning-up' in oven.

3 Cook 6 to 8 minutes or until water just comes up to boil, turning dish twice. Stand for 5 minutes.

4 Remove from dish with perforated fish slice and stand on individual plates. Serve hot with hollandaise sauce (see Sauce section) or cold with mayonnaise.

Note: do not freeze after cooking.

Kedgeree (Serves 4)

Ingredients	Imperial	American
350g smoked haddock fillet	12oz	12oz
50g butter	2oz	¼ cup
50g onion	2oz	1 small
225g Easy cook long grain rice	8oz	1¼ cups
575ml or 6dl boiling water	1pt	2½ cups
2 x grade 3 hard-boiled eggs	2 standard	2 medium hard-cooked
salt and pepper to taste	to taste	to taste
2 x 15ml level tbsp chopped parsley	2 level tbsp	3 level tbsp

1 Place smoked haddock fillet in glass or pottery dish. Cover with cling film, making 2 slits in it with scissors to prevent it from 'ballooning-up' in oven. Cook 4 minutes, half turning dish after 2 minutes. Flake fish, discarding any skin and bones.

2 In fairly deep dish, melt butter for 2 minutes in the microwave. Chop onion finely. Add to dish. Cook, uncovered, 4 minutes.

3 Stir in rice and water. Cover dish with lid or cling film. (If using film, make 2 slits in it with scissors to prevent it from 'ballooning-up' in oven.) Cook in microwave 15 minutes, half turning dish after 7½ minutes.

4 Leave to stand 10 minutes. Uncover. Stir in 1 chopped egg and seasoning to taste. Fork in fish. Warm through, uncovered, 4 minutes. Half turn dish after 2 minutes.

5 Slice second egg. Garnish kedgeree with egg slices and chopped parsley.

Note: do not freeze.

Tuna fish pie (Serves 4 to 6)

Ingredients	Imperial	American
¾kg freshly boiled and mashed potatoes	1½lb	24oz
100g canned tuna	7oz	1 cup
1 x 5ml level tsp salt	1 level tsp	1½ level tsp
1 x 5ml level tsp dried tarragon	1 level tsp	1½ level tsp
2 x 5ml level tsp prepared mild mustard	2 level tsp	3 level tsp
4 x 15ml level tbsp chopped parsley	4 level tbsp	6 level tbsp
1 x grade 3 egg, beaten	1 standard	1 medium
1 x 5ml level tsp paprika	1 level tsp	1½ level tsp

1 Place potatoes in large bowl. Add mashed tuna (plus oil from can) together with all remaining ingredients except paprika. Mix thoroughly.

2 Transfer to medium-sized glass or pottery dish, first greased with butter. Ridge top with prongs of a fork then sprinkle with paprika.

3 Cook, uncovered, in microwave for 7 minutes, half turning dish after 3½ minutes. Leave to stand 5 minutes then serve with sauce to taste (see Sauce section), and a green vegetable.

Note: this dish is suitable for freezing.

Curried fish pie (Serves 4 to 6)

Make exactly as above, adding 2 to 3 x 15ml level tablespoons (2 to 3 level tablespoons or American 3 to 4) curry paste. Before serving, sprinkle with chopped hard egg.

Prawns provençale (Serves 6)

Ingredients	Imperial	American
25g butter	1oz	⅛ cup
1 large garlic clove	1 large	1 large
250ml or 3dl canned tomatoes, crushed	½pt	1¼ cups
1 x 5ml level tsp dried oregano	1 level tsp	1½ level tsp
1 x 5ml level tsp salt	1 level tsp	1½ level tsp
½kg frozen peeled prawns	1lb	16oz
2 x 15ml level tbsp chopped fresh parsley	2 level tbsp	3 level tbsp

1 Melt butter, uncovered, in medium-sized casserole dish. Allow between 1 and 2 minutes. Meanwhile chop garlic finely. Add to melted butter and stir round. Cover. Cook 2 minutes.

2 Stir in tomatoes, oregano and salt. Cover with lid or cling film. (If using film, make 2 slits in it with scissors to prevent it from 'ballooning-up' in oven.) Cook 5 minutes.

3 Add prawns. Cover. Cook 3 minutes. Stir well, carefully separating prawns if necessary. Cover. Cook further 3 to 4 minutes or until piping hot.

4 Sprinkle with parsley and accompany with freshly boiled rice.

Note: do not freeze.

5 Meat and Poultry

Although I was warned before I started this book that some casserole-type meat dishes—made from the less tender cuts—would not respond well to microwave cooking, I found I could resolve the problem almost completely by:

1 Cutting the meat into smaller-than-usual pieces.

2 Cooking it covered but *without water*—or liquid of any sort—for the first 15 to 20 minutes. This has the effect of softening the meat or poultry, with the result that cooking can be completed in under 30 minutes for most dishes.

3 Adding most of the salt-based seasonings at the end.

Note: kosher meat, eaten by the Jewish community, is impregnated with salt before it is cooked, so it is difficult to guarantee that it will become fully tender under microwave conditions.

Defrosting meat and poultry

1 Frozen meat and poultry should be completely thawed before cooking. This can be done either by leaving food in the refrigerator overnight or defrosting in the microwave. The former method is best for larger-than-average joints and poultry.

2 In order to prevent uneven cooking, protect legs and wings of poultry, together with thin ends of roasts, with aluminium foil during defrosting in the microwave. This will shield these portions from microwave energy.

3 Foods covered with paper, or placed in a roasting bag, will defrost more quickly in the microwave and also retain more moisture.

4 For even penetration of microwave energy, food should be rotated halfway through the defrosting period otherwise, after cooking, some small areas may be over-cooked.

5 Steaks, chops, sausages and chicken pieces in the microwave should be separated and placed in a single layer as soon as possible after defrosting begins, turning

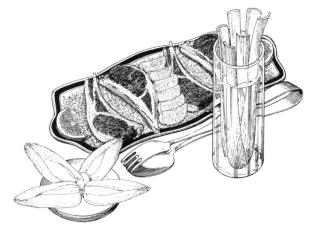

if necessary for even energy penetration halfway through defrosting.

6 When defrosting minced meat, remove the soft defrosted portions as soon as possible and only return the frozen portion to the microwave.

7 Meat and poultry require standing time in between periods of heating to prevent food from cooking on the outside before the middle has thawed completely.

Roast chicken   Poultry needs only eight minutes to the lb (or $\frac{1}{2}$kg) in the microwave.

Meat defrosting chart (for ovens with a defrost switch or power control dial)

	Quantity or weight	Set Timer for	Leave to stand for	Set timer for	Leave to stand for
Beef					
Joints for roasting, ie topside, sirloin	1$\frac{1}{2}$kg (3lb)	10 mins	20 mins	5 mins	20 mins
Rolled joints	1$\frac{1}{2}$kg (3lb)	10 mins	20 mins	5 mins	10 mins
Stewing or braising meat	1kg (2lb)	5 mins	10 mins	2$\frac{1}{2}$ mins	5 mins
Grilling steak	1$\frac{1}{2}$kg (3lb)	5 mins	10 mins	5 mins	10 mins
Individual grilling steaks	125–225g (4-8 oz)	5 mins	15 mins	4 mins	10 mins
Minced beef	$\frac{1}{2}$kg (1lb)	5 mins	10 mins	2$\frac{1}{2}$ mins	
Pork					
Sausagemeat	$\frac{1}{2}$kg (1lb)	2$\frac{1}{2}$ mins	10 mins	2$\frac{1}{2}$ mins	
Roast loin	1$\frac{1}{2}$kg (3lb)	10 mins	20 mins	5 mins	10 mins
Roast leg	2$\frac{1}{2}$kg (5lb)	10 mins	30 mins	5 mins	20 mins
Chops	2	2$\frac{1}{2}$ mins	5 mins	2$\frac{1}{2}$ mins	
	4	5 mins	10 mins	2$\frac{1}{2}$ mins	5 mins
Poultry					
Chicken	1kg (2lb)	10 mins	20 mins	5 mins	10 mins
	1$\frac{1}{2}$kg (3lb)	10 mins	20 mins	5 mins	10 mins
Chicken pieces	200–225g (8–9oz) each	5 mins	10 mins	2$\frac{1}{2}$ mins	10 mins
Turkey	6kg (13lb)	20 mins	30 mins	10 mins	20 mins
Lamb					
Roast leg	2$\frac{1}{2}$kg (5lb)	10 mins	20 mins	5 mins	10 mins
Chops	2	2$\frac{1}{2}$ mins	5 mins	2$\frac{1}{2}$ mins	
	4	5 mins	10 mins	2$\frac{1}{2}$ mins	5 mins
Veal					
Roast shoulder or leg	1$\frac{1}{2}$kg (3lb)	5 mins	10 mins	5 mins	10 mins
	2$\frac{1}{2}$kg (5lb)	10 mins	20 mins	5 mins	10 mins
Casseroles	1 litre (1$\frac{3}{4}$pt)	10 mins	20 mins	5 mins	
	2 litre (3$\frac{1}{2}$pt)	10 mins	20 mins	5 mins	10 mins

Defrosting times

A defrosting chart is *only applicable* to a microwave with a pulse unit or automatically-controlled defrost switch. If you have neither of these, treat meat and poultry in the following way:

Small portions of meat and poultry up to 1kg (2lb)

Heat 2 minutes. Rest 2 minutes. Heat 1 minute. Rest 2 minutes. Heat 1 minute. Rest 2 minutes. Heat 1 minute. Rest 2 minutes. Heat 1 minute. Rest 5-10 minutes or until food has obviously thawed and feels slightly warm to the touch. Separate chops and steaks, etc as soon as possible to speed up defrosting.

Portions of meat and poultry up to 1$\frac{1}{2}$kg (3lb)

Treat as above, allowing a further 3 x 1 minute heating time with 2 minute rest periods between.

Joints of meat and whole poultry up to 2kg (just over 4lb)

Treat as meat and poultry up to 1½kg (3lb) but allow a further 4 to 5 x 1 minute heating time with 2 minute rest periods between.

If some cooking occurs on the outside edges while defrosting large pieces of meat and poultry, this is perfectly acceptable provided the food is to be cooked immediately. To avoid this happening at all, use more shorter heating times with longer resting times in between. For this reason, larger joints and birds are best if left to defrost in the refrigerator overnight.

Cooking meat and poultry

A joint will have a better appearance and will cook more evenly if it is a regular shape. Ideal cuts are top leg of pork or lamb or rolled joints. However, if the joint is not uniform in size, the narrower section should be covered with a smooth piece of foil for the first half of the cooking period. If the joint is more than 12.5cm (5in) thick, allow it to stand for 30 minutes halfway through the cooking period. Poultry should have the wings and legs tied closely to the body and covered with foil. (See page 47.)

Instructions for cooking

1   Roasting bags are ideal for cooking all joints in the microwave. Season the joint and place in the roasting bag. Loosely seal the neck and place in the oven. Cook for the time stated on the chart and then leave to rest or stand for 20-30 minutes, when cooking will be completed. If the joint is left in the roasting bag for this period it will retain all its surface heat and will be the correct temperature for serving. Alternatively, joints can be 'open' cooked in a dish or on a plate and covered with kitchen paper or grease proof (wax) paper to help prevent grease splashing on to the oven interior.

2   If the use of a trivet is preferred, place a small flat dish inside a roasting dish as or use 1 or 2 inverted saucers.

3   If the joint has fat on one side only, place it fat side down at the commencement of cooking and turn halfway through the cooking period.

4   Add salt, pepper or other seasonings if desired. If the total cooking time is 15 minutes or more, the joint will brown naturally. For extra browning, the joint may be placed in a conventional oven at a high setting for 10-15 minutes at the end of the cooking period.

5   After cooking, cover the meat in foil to retain heat during the rest period or place in a conventional oven for extra browning.

Note: for crisp crackling on pork, score fat deeply with a sharp knife then sprinkle heavily with salt. Cook 'open' as described above under Point 1.

Meat and poultry roasting chart

The times for roasting given below are for joints of meat, etc at room temperature. If taken straight from the refrigerator, allow an extra 1 to 2 minutes per ½kg (1lb).

Meat		Minutes per ½kg (1lb)
Beef, rolled rib, rump	rare	6 mins
	medium	7 mins
	well done	8 mins
Pork		9 mins
Ham		9 mins
Lamb		9 mins
Veal		9 mins
Poultry		8 mins

Traditional mince (Serves 4)

Ingredients	Imperial	American
½kg minced beef, lean	1lb	16oz
1 medium onion	1 medium	1 medium
2 x 15ml level tbsp plain flour	2 level tbsp	3 level tbsp
425ml or 4dl hot water	¾pt	1½ cups
1 x 5ml level tsp salt	1 level tsp	1 level tsp
1 brown gravy cube	1	1

1   Place mince in large but fairly shallow dish. Finely grate onion. Add to mince with flour. Fork-mix thoroughly. Cook, uncovered, 5 minutes.
2   Break up meat with fork then stir in water and salt. Crumble gravy cube over top. Stir well to mix.
3   Cover with lid or cling film.(If using cling film, make 2 slits in it with scissors to prevent it from 'ballooning-up' in oven.) Cook ¼ hour, half turning dish after 7½ minutes.
4   Leave to rest 5 minutes, stir round, then serve with creamed or boiled potatoes and vegetables to taste.

Note: this dish is suitable for deep freezing.

Shepherd's pie (Serves 4)

Make traditional mince as directed above. Cover with ¾kg (1½lb or 24oz American) freshly boiled potatoes creamed with 25g (1oz or ⅛ cup American) butter or margarine and 4 x 15ml tablespoons (4 tablespoons or American 6 tablespoons) hot milk. Season to taste. Brown quickly under a hot grill or in hot oven.

Scottish-style mince (Serves 4)

Ingredients	Imperial	American
½kg minced beef, lean	1lb	16oz
1 medium onion	1 medium	1 medium
2 x 5ml level tbsp mixed dried vegetables	2 level tbsp	3 level tbsp
25g rolled oats	1oz	about ½ cup
425ml or 4dl hot water	¾pt	1½ cups
1 brown gravy cube	1	1
1 x 5ml level tsp salt	1 level tsp	1½ level tsp

1   Place mince in large but fairly shallow dish. Finely grate onion. Add to mince with dried vegetables. Fork-mix thoroughly. Cook, uncovered, 5 minutes.

Beef stew (Serves 4)

Ingredients	Imperial	American
½kg stewing beef, lean	1lb	16oz
1 x 15ml level tbsp plain flour	1 level tbsp	1½ level tbsp
250g frozen vegetable stew pack, unthawed	½lb	1 medium pack
275ml or 3dl boiling water	½pt	1¼ cups
1 brown gravy cube	1	1
½ to 1 x 5ml level tsp salt	½ level tsp	¾ level tsp

1   Cut meat into 1¼cm (½in) cubes. Place, in single layer, in large but fairly shallow dish. Sprinkle flour over meat then toss over and over with a spoon.
2   Make sure meat remains in single layer. Surround with vegetables. Cover with lid or cling film. (If using film, make 2 slits in it with scissors to prevent it from 'ballooning-up' in oven.)
3   Cook ¼ hour, half turning dish after 7½ minutes. Pour water into jug, crumble in gravy cube and stir until dissolved. Uncover meat, pour in water and stir well.
4   Cover with lid or film (making slits in film as before). Cook 10 minutes, half turning dish after 5 minutes. Stir in salt. Serve with creamed potatoes and green vegetables to taste.

Note: this dish is suitable for deep freezing.

2   Break up meat with fork and stir in rolled oats and water. Crumble gravy cube over top. Sprinkle with salt then mix thoroughly.

3   Cover with lid or cling film. (If using film, make 2 slits in it with scissors to prevent it from 'ballooning-up' in oven.) Cook ¼ hour, half turning dish after 7½ minutes.

4   Leave to rest for 5 minutes, stir round, then serve with creamed potatoes and vegetables to taste.

Note: this dish is suitable for deep freezing.

Easy chili con carne (Serves 4 to 5)

Ingredients	Imperial	American
½kg minced beef, lean	1lb	16oz
1 medium onion	1 medium	1 medium
2 medium garlic cloves	2 medium	2 medium
3 x 5ml level tsp chili seasoning	3 level tsp	4½ level tsp
½kg size canned tomatoes	1lb size	2 cups
1 x 5ml level tsp salt	1 level tsp	1½ level tsp
2 x 5ml tsp Worcester sauce	2 tsp	3 tsp
½kg size canned red kidney beans	1lb size	16oz size

1   Place mince in large but fairly shallow dish. Finely chop onion and garlic. Add to mince. Fork-mix thoroughly. Cook, uncovered, 5 minutes.

2   Break up meat with fork then stir in chili seasoning, canned tomatoes (first broken down by crushing with spoon), salt, Worcester sauce and drained kidney beans. Fork-stir well to mix.

3   Cover with lid or film. (If using film, make 2 slits in it with scissors to prevent it from 'ballooning-up' in oven.)

4   Cook ¼ hour, half turning dish after 7½ minutes. Leave to rest 5 minutes, stir round, then serve with freshly cooked rice.

Notes: chili seasoning is made up of a special blend of fairly mild spices which are purplish-brown in colour. It should not be confused with Cayenne pepper which is dark red and extremely fiery; nor with sweet paprika which has a distinctive but gentle flavour.
This dish is suitable for deep freezing.

Meatballs neapolitan (Serves 4)

Ingredients	Imperial	American
2 x 15ml tbsp olive oil	2 tbsp	3 tbsp
1 medium onion	1 medium	1 medium
2 medium garlic cloves	2 medium	2 medium
½kg minced beef, lean	1lb	16oz ground beef
4 x 15ml rounded tbsp fresh white breadcrumbs	4 rounded tbsp	6 rounded tbsp
1 x grade 3 egg	1 standard	1 medium
2 x 5ml level tsp salt	2 level tsp	3 level tsp
½kg size canned tomatoes	about 1lb size	2 cups
1 x 5ml level tsp brown sugar	1 level tsp	1½ level tsp
1 x 5ml level tsp dried basil or oregano	1 level tsp	1½ level tsp

1   Pour olive oil into a large but fairly shallow dish. Finely chop onion and garlic. Add to oil. Stir well to mix. Cook, uncovered, 4 minutes.

2   Meanwhile, make meatballs. Combine beef with crumbs, beaten egg and half the salt. Shape into 12 small balls. Add to dish. Cook, uncovered 2½ minutes. Turn meatballs over. Cook, uncovered, a further 2½ minutes. Leave to rest temporarily.

3   Crush tomatoes or blend in blender goblet until smooth. Add rest of salt with sugar and basil or oregano. Pour over meatballs.

4   Cover with lid or cling film. (If using film, make 2 slits in it with scissors to prevent it from 'ballooning-up' in oven.) Cook 10 minutes, half turning dish after 5 minutes.

5   Serve with freshly cooked pasta and butter-fried courgettes or a mixed salad.

Note: this dish is suitable for deep freezing.

Beef 'hot-pot' (Serves 4)

Ingredients	Imperial	American
½kg potatoes, peeled	1lb	16oz
1 large onion, peeled	1 large	1 large
½kg stewing beef, lean	1lb	16oz
1 brown gravy cube	1	1
125ml or 1¼dl boiling water	¼pt	⅝ cup
15g butter or margarine	½oz	2 tsp

1 Wash and dry potatoes and cut into wafer-thin slices. Coarsely grate onions. Cut meat into 1¼cm (½in) cubes.

2 Place layers of potatoes, onions and meat in large but fairly shallow dish, beginning and ending with potatoes.

3 Cover with lid or cling film. (If using film, cut 2 slits in it with scissors to prevent it from 'ballooning-up' in oven.) Cook ¼ hour, giving dish a half turn after 7½ minutes.

4 Uncover. Crumble gravy cube into water, stir until dissolved then carefully pour into dish over vegetables and meat.

5 Top with flakes of butter or margarine, cover dish with lid or film (making slits in film as before) and cook ¼ hour, half turning dish after 7½ minutes.

6 Serve hot with green vegetables to taste.

Note: this dish is suitable for brief deep freezing; up to about 1 month.

Beef curry (Serves 4 to 5)

Ingredients	Imperial	American
½kg stewing beef, lean	1lb	16oz
2 medium onions	2 medium	2 medium
2 garlic cloves	2	2
2 x 15ml tbsp salad oil	2 tbsp	3 tbsp
2 x 15ml level tbsp Madras curry powder	2 level tbsp	3 level tbsp
2 x 15ml level tbsp tomato purée	2 level tbsp	3 level tbsp
1 x 15ml level tbsp plain flour	2 level tbsp	3 level tbsp
4 green cardamoms	4	4
1 x 5ml level tsp ground ginger	1 level tsp	1½ level tsp
2 x 5ml level tsp ground cummin seed (jeera)	2 level tsp	3 level tsp
2 small bay leaves	2 small	2 small
425ml or 4dl hot water	¾pt	2 cups
1 x 5ml level tsp salt	1 level tsp	1½ level tsp

1 Cut meat into 1¼cm (½in) cubes. Place, in single layer, in large but fairly shallow dish. Cover with lid or cling film. (If using film, cut 2 slits in it with scissors to prevent it from 'ballooning-up' in oven.) Cook ¼ hour, giving dish a half turn after 7½ minutes.

2 Fry onions and garlic conventionally in oil until deep gold. Keep lid on pan and heat medium. Stir in curry powder, tomato purée, flour, cardamoms, ginger, cummin seed and bay leaves.

3 Gradually blend in hot water. Add salt. Cook, stirring, until sauce comes to boil and thickens. Remove meat from oven and uncover. Pour sauce into dish. Mix well with meat.

4 Cover dish with lid or film (making slits in film as before). Cook 10 minutes, half turning dish after 5 minutes.

5 Serve with freshly boiled Indian rice and sambals (side dishes) of mango chutney, chopped raw onion, toasted coconut, yogurt and sliced tomatoes.

Note: this dish is suitable for deep freezing.

Boeuf bourguignon (Serves 4)

Ingredients	Imperial	American
½kg stewing beef, lean	1lb	16oz
25g butter or margarine	1oz	⅛ cup
1 large onion, chopped	1 large	1 large
2 large garlic cloves, chopped	2 large	2 large
125g mild and lean bacon, chopped	4oz	½ cup
125g trimmed button mushrooms	4oz	1¼ cups
1 x 15ml level tbsp plain flour	1 level tbsp	1½ level tbsp
425ml or 4dl Burgundy	¾pt	2 cups
1 x 5ml level tsp salt	1 level tsp	1½ level tsp

1 Cut meat into 1¼cm (½in) cubes. Place butter or margarine in large but fairly shallow dish. Melt, uncovered, about 1 minute. Add meat, onion, garlic, bacon and mushrooms.

2 Toss round and round in the butter or margarine with a spoon, then spread meat and vegetables, etc over base of dish to form a single layer.

3 Cover with lid or cling film. (If using film, cut 2 slits in it with scissors to prevent it from 'ballooning-up' in oven.) Cook ¼ hour, half turning dish after 7½ minutes.

4 Meanwhile, mix flour smoothly with the wine, whisking if necessary to remove small lumps. Add salt.

5 When meat is ready, uncover then pour wine mixture into dish over meat and vegetables. Stir thoroughly to combine. Cover with lid or film (making slits in film as before). Cook 10 minutes, half turning dish after 5 minutes.

6 Leave to rest for 5 minutes then serve with whole boiled potatoes tossed in butter and sprinkled with chopped parsley. Accompany with green vegetables or mixed salad.

Note: this dish is suitable for deep freezing.

Belgian beef in beer (Serves 4)

Ingredients	Imperial	American
½kg stewing beef, lean	1lb	16oz
25g butter or margarine	1oz	⅛ cup
2 large onions, chopped	2 large	2 large
2 large garlic cloves, chopped	2 large	2 large
2 x 5ml level tsp soft brown sugar (dark variety)	2 level tsp	3 level tsp
275ml or 3dl Guinness or other dark beer	½pt	1¼ cups
1 x 5ml level tsp salt	1 level tsp	1½ level tsp
3 x 15ml heaped tbsp soft white breadcrumbs	3 heaped tbsp	4½ heaped tbsp

1 Cut meat into 1¼cm (½in) cubes. Place butter or margarine in large but fairly shallow dish. Melt, uncovered, about 1 minute. Add meat, onions, garlic and sugar.

2 Toss round and round in the butter or margarine with a spoon then spread meat and onions, etc over base of dish to form a single layer.

3 Cover dish with lid or cling film. (If using film, cut 2 slits in it with scissors to prevent it from 'ballooning-up' in oven.) Cook ¼ hour, half turning dish after 7½ minutes.

4 Pour beer into dish over meat and vegetables. Sprinkle with salt. Stir thoroughly to combine. Cover with lid or film (making slits in film as before). Cook 20 minutes, half turning dish after 10 minutes.

5 Uncover then stir in breadcrumbs to thicken. If gravy is still too thin for personal taste, add 1 or 2 extra tablespoons of crumbs.

6 Serve with freshly boiled potatoes and cabbage or sprouts tossed in butter.

Note: this dish is suitable for deep freezing.

Beef goulash (Serves 6)

Ingredients	Imperial	American
¾kg stewing steak	1½lb	1½lb
40g butter or margarine	1½oz	3 tbsp
225g onions	8oz	2 medium
125g green pepper	4oz	1 medium
2 medium garlic cloves	2 medium	2 medium
225g skinned and chopped tomatoes	8oz	1 cup
3 x 15ml level tbsp tomato purée	3 level tbsp	4½ level tbsp
1 x 15ml level tbsp paprika	1 level tbsp	1½ level tbsp
1 x 5ml level tsp salt	1 level tsp	1½ level tsp
½ x 5ml level tsp caraway seeds	½ level tsp	¾ level tsp
125ml or 1½dl soured cream	¼pt	⅝ cup

1 Cut meat into 1¼cm (½in) cubes. Place butter or margarine in large but fairly shallow glass or pottery dish. Melt 1½ minutes in microwave. Add meat.

2 Finely chop onions, de-seeded green pepper and garlic. Add to dish. Stir well to mix. Cover with lid or cling film. (If using film, make 2 slits in it with scissors to prevent it from 'ballooning-up' in oven.) Cook ¼ hour, half turning dish after 7½ minutes.

3 Uncover. Stir in all remaining ingredients except cream. Mix thoroughly. Cover with lid or film (making 2 slits in film as before).

4 Cook 20 minutes, giving dish a quarter turn every 5 minutes. Leave to stand 5 minutes. Uncover. Stir in cream. Serve with freshly boiled potatoes or ribbon noodles and green vegetables to taste.

Note: the goulash is suitable for deep freezing, provided soured cream is omitted. This should be stirred in after thawing and reheating.

Chicken curry with coconut Chicken joints in delicious curry sauce, served with rice, coconut, chutney, lemon slices, yoghurt, cucumber and tomatoes. (Recipe page 63)

Meat loaf (Serves 4 to 6)

Ingredients	Imperial	American
½kg minced beef, lean	1lb	16oz ground beef
25g pack onion white sauce mix	1oz	for 1¼ cups milk
125ml or 1½dl cold milk	¼pt	⅝ cup
1 x 5ml level tsp dry mustard	1 level tsp	1½ level tsp
1 x 5ml level tsp dried mixed herbs	1 level tsp	1½ level tsp
1 x 15ml tbsp tomato ketchup	1 tbsp	1½ tbsp
1 x 15ml level tbsp soft brown sugar (dark variety)	1 level tbsp	1½ level tbsp

1   Well grease a ¾l (1½pt or 4 cup American) oval pie dish. In large bowl, combine beef with all remaining ingredients except sugar. Mixture will appear slack but firms-up on cooking.
2   Press evenly into pie dish. Sprinkle with sugar. Cover with cling film, making 2 slits in it with scissors to prevent it from 'ballooning-up' in oven.
3   Cook 7 minutes, half turning dish after 3½ minutes. Leave to stand 5 minutes. Cut into slices and serve hot with baked jacket potatoes and either a salad or green vegetables.

Note: leftover loaf may be deep frozen for up to about 2 months.

Irish stew (Serves 3 to 4)

Ingredients	Imperial	American
¾kg stewing lamb (with bone)	1½lb	24oz
½kg potatoes, peeled	1lb	16oz
2 large onions, peeled	2 large	2 large
275ml or 3dl boiling water	½pt	1¼ cups
1 x 5ml level tsp salt	1 level tsp	1½ level tsp
2 x 15ml level tbsp parsley, chopped	2 level tbsp	3 level tbsp

1   Have butcher cut lamb into large cubes. Trim away surplus fat and discard. Cut potatoes into small dice. Coarsely grate onions.
2   Place meat and vegetables, in even layer, in large but fairly shallow dish. Cover with lid or cling film. (If using film, cut 2 slits in it with scissors to prevent it from 'ballooning-up' in oven.) Cook ¼ hour, half turning dish after 7½ minutes. Take out of microwave and uncover.
3   Mix water and salt together. Pour into dish over meat and vegetables. Stir thoroughly to combine. Cover with lid or film (making slits in film as before). Cook 20 minutes, half turning dish after 10 minutes.
4   Leave to rest for 10 minutes then uncover and sprinkle with parsley.

Note: this dish can be frozen for up to 2 months.

Lamb chops boulangère (Serves 4)

Ingredients	Imperial	American
250g cold cooked potatoes	½lb	8oz
250g cold cooked carrots	½lb	8oz
4 lamb chump chops, each 100 to 150g	each 4 to 5oz	each 4 to 5oz
1 small onion, peeled and grated	1 small	1 small
1 medium cooking apple	1 medium	1 medium
15g butter or margarine	½oz	1 tbsp
salt and pepper to taste	to taste	to taste

1   Slice potatoes and carrots very thinly and arrange in single layer over base of large but fairly shallow dish.
2   Stand chops on top then sprinkle with grated onion. Peel apple, cut into thin slices then arrange on top of onion.
3   Dot with flakes of butter or margarine, sprinkle with salt and pepper then cover dish with lid or cling film. (If using film, make 2 slits in it with scissors to prevent it from 'ballooning-up' in oven.)
4   Cook ¼ hour, half turning dish after 7½ minutes. Leave to rest 5 minutes then serve chops with green peas or sprouts tossed in butter.

Note: this dish is suitable for deep freezing.

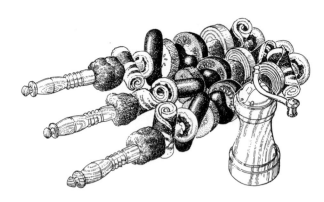

Lamb kebabs (Serves 6)

Ingredients	Imperial	American
¾kg lamb fillet (cut from leg)	1½lb	1½lb
Baste		
25g butter or margarine	1oz	⅛ cup
1 x 5ml level tsp garlic salt	1 level tsp	1½ level tsp
1 x 5ml level tsp paprika	1 level tsp	1½ level tsp
1 x 5ml tsp soy sauce	1 level tsp	1½ level tsp

1   Cut lamb fillet into 2½cm (1in) cubes. Thread onto 6 metal skewers, each 10cm (4in) long.

2   Arrange, like spokes of a wheel, on large dinner plate.

3   To make baste, place butter or margarine in small dish. Melt 1 minute in microwave. Stir in remaining ingredients.

4   Brush over kebabs. Cook, uncovered, 5 minutes. Half turn plate after 2½ minutes. Remove from oven. Turn kebabs over. Brush with rest of baste. Cook further 5 minutes, half turning plate as before.

5   Serve with warm pitta bread or on a bed of freshly cooked rice. Accompany, Greek-style, with wedges of lemon and a large mixed salad.

Note: do not freeze.

Persian lamb (Serves 4)

Ingredients	Imperial	American
1½kg shoulder of lamb	3lb	3lb
1 x 5ml level tsp ground cinnamon	1 level tsp	1½ level tsp
1 x 5ml level tsp ground cloves	1 level tsp	1½ level tsp
2 x 15ml level tbsp soft brown sugar	2 level tbsp	3 level tbsp
75g onion	3oz	1 small to medium
2 x 15ml tbsp lemon juice	2 tbsp	3 tbsp
¼ x 5ml level tsp white pepper	¼ level tsp	½ level tsp
2 x 5ml level tsp cornflour	2 level tsp	3 level tsp cornstarch
1 x 15ml level tbsp water	1 level tbsp	1½ level tbsp
½ x 5ml level tsp salt	½ level tsp	¾ level tsp
About ½kg canned peach slices	15½oz	2 cups
25g butter	1oz	⅛ cup
150ml natural yogurt	¼pt	⅝ cup

1   Bone shoulder and cut meat into $1\frac{1}{4}$cm ($\frac{1}{2}$in) cubes. Place in fairly shallow glass or pottery dish.

2   Mix together cinnamon, cloves and sugar. Sprinkle over meat. Stir well to mix. Sprinkle with finely chopped onion, lemon juice and pepper. Cover with paper towel. Cook 5 minutes and rest 5 minutes. Repeat 3 times, stirring after each rest period.

3   Mix cornflour to cream with water. Drain liquid from lamb and blend into cornflour mixture with salt. Pour over lamb. Mix well. Cook, uncovered, further $1\frac{1}{2}$ minutes.

4   Gently stir in drained peach slices. Cook, uncovered, further $1\frac{1}{2}$ minutes.

5   Accompany with the yogurt, plain boiled rice and a lettuce salad.

Note: this dish is suitable for deep freezing.

Aubergine moussaka (Serves 6)

Ingredients	Imperial	American
25g butter	1oz	$\frac{1}{8}$ cup
225g onions, finely chopped	8oz	2 large
$\frac{1}{2}$kg cooked minced lamb or beef	1lb	3 cups
225g skinned and chopped tomatoes	8oz	1 cup
2 x 15ml level tbsp tomato purée	2 level tbsp	3 level tbsp
2 x 15ml tbsp stock or water	2 tbsp	3 tbsp
1 x 5ml level tsp salt	1 level tsp	$1\frac{1}{2}$ level tsp
$\frac{3}{4}$kg aubergines	$1\frac{1}{2}$lb	2 large eggplants
4 x 15ml tbsp white wine	4 tbsp	6 tbsp
275ml or 3dl basic white sauce	$\frac{1}{2}$pt	$1\frac{1}{4}$ cups
1 x grade 3 egg	1 standard	1 medium
4 x 15ml level tbsp grated Parmesan cheese	4 level tbsp	6 level tbsp

1   Melt butter in glass or pottery dish for 1 minute in the microwave. Add onions. Cook, uncovered, 2 minutes. Stir in meat, tomatoes, tomato pureé, stock or water and the salt.

2   Wash and dry aubergines but do not peel. Slice fairly thinly. Place in large saucepan and cover with boiling water. Poach conventionally for 2 minutes. Drain.

3   Fill a large glass or pottery dish with alternate layers of meat mixture and aubergines. Sprinkle over the wine.

4   To the hot white sauce, add the beaten egg and half the cheese. Stir well to mix. Adjust seasoning to taste.

5   Pour over moussaka mixture and sprinkle with rest of cheese. Cook, uncovered, 10 to 15 minutes in the microwave until very hot. Half turn dish after 5 or $7\frac{1}{2}$ minutes.

Note: this dish is suitable for deep freezing.

Potato moussaka

When aubergines are out of season, substitute the same amount of cooked potatoes.

Pork chops with sauerkraut (Serves 4)

Ingredients	Imperial	American
$\frac{1}{2}$kg sauerkraut	1lb	1lb
4 medium canned or fresh skinned tomatoes	4 medium	4 medium
2 x 5ml level tsp salt	2 level tsp	3 level tsp
4 pork chops, each 175 to 225g	6 to 8oz	large
2 x 5ml tsp soy sauce	2 tsp	3 tsp
garlic salt and paprika to sprinkle	to sprinkle	to sprinkle
1 x 15ml level tbsp soft brown sugar (dark variety)	1 level tbsp	$1\frac{1}{2}$ level tbsp

1   Place sauerkraut in a colander and wash under cold, running water to reduce excess acidity. Drain thoroughly, pressing sauerkraut against sides of colander with a wooden spoon.

2   Arrange, in single layer, in large but fairly shallow glass or pottery dish. Add tomatoes and salt. Stir well to mix.

3   Place chops on top of sauerkraut then pour soy sauce over each. Sprinkle with garlic salt, paprika and soft brown sugar.

4   Cover with lid or cling film. (If using film, make 2 slits in it with scissors to prevent it from 'ballooning-up' in oven.) Cook $\frac{1}{4}$ hour, half turning dish after $7\frac{1}{2}$ minutes.

Aubergine moussaka   Simple, impressive and surprisingly
quick to make. (Recipe page 59)

Meat and Poultry   **61**

5   Leave to rest 10 minutes then serve with freshly creamed potatoes.

Note: this dish is suitable for deep freezing.

Sweet-sour pork chops (Serves 4)

Ingredients	Imperial	American
4 pork chops, fat-trimmed, each 150g after trimming	each 5–6oz after trimming	each 5–6oz after trimming
4 x 15ml level tbsp tomato ketchup	4 level tbsp	6 level tbsp
1 x 15ml tbsp soy sauce	1 tbsp	1½ tbsp
4 x 5ml tsp vinegar	4 tsp	6 tsp
1 small orange, peeled	1 small	1 small
¼ x 5ml level tsp garlic salt	¼ level tsp	just over ¼ level tsp

1   Arrange chops, side by side, in large but fairly shallow dish.
2   Mix together ketchup, soy sauce and vinegar. Add diced orange and garlic salt. Stir well to mix.
3   Spoon over chops. Cover with lid or cling film. (If using film, make 2 slits in it with scissors to prevent it from 'ballooning-up' in oven.)
4   Cook 12 minutes, giving dish a quarter turn every 3 minutes. Leave to rest 5 minutes then serve with freshly cooked rice. A salad of chicory and celery teams well with the chops.

Note: this dish can be deep frozen.

Barbecue-style spare ribs (Serves 4)

Ingredients	Imperial	American
16 Chinese style pork spare ribs	16	16
2 x 15ml tbsp lemon juice	2 tbsp	3 tbsp
2½ x 15ml tbsp soy sauce	2½ tbsp	3¼ tbsp
½ x 5ml level tsp dried horseradish	½ level tsp	¾ level tsp
2 x 5ml tsp Worcester sauce	2 tsp	3 tsp
¼ x 5ml level tsp of each of salt and pepper	¼ level tsp of each	½ level tsp of each
275ml or 3dl orange juice	½pt	1¼ cups
1 x 5ml level tsp dry mustard	1 level tsp	1½ level tsp
2 x 15ml level tbsp soft brown sugar	2 level tbsp	3 level tbsp
1 large garlic clove	1 large	1 large

1   Place spare ribs into fairly shallow glass or pottery dish. Cover with cling film, making 2 slits in it with scissors to prevent it from 'ballooning-up' in oven. Cook 7 minutes, half turning dish after 3½ minutes.
2   Uncover. Drain off fat. Beat rest of ingredients well together or blend until smooth in liquidiser goblet.
3   Pour over ribs. Cover with kitchen paper. Cook 20 minutes, giving dish a quarter turn every 5 minutes and basting with barbecue sauce in dish.
4   Serve with freshly cooked rice and accompany with lemon wedges.

Veal fricassée (Serves 6)

Follow recipe for Chicken Fricassée (page 63) but substitute 1½lb (¾kg or 24oz American) lean stewing veal for the chicken. Cut into 1¼cm (½in) cubes and place in dish as directed. Cooking times are exactly the same.

Note: this dish can be deep frozen.

Piquant veal chops (Serves 4)

Ingredients	Imperial	American
25g butter	1oz	⅛ cup
1 x 5ml level tsp sweet paprika	1 level tsp	1½ level tsp
1 x 5ml tsp soy sauce	1 tsp	1½ tsp
1 x 5ml tsp Worcester sauce	1 tsp	1½ tsp
4 veal chops, each 125 to 150g	each 5oz	each 5oz

1   Place butter in large but shallow dish. Melt 1 minute in microwave. Stir in paprika, soy and Worcester sauces.
2   Stand chops in dish. Turn over so that both sides are evenly coated with butter mixture.
3   Cover with lid or cling film. (If using film, make 2 slits in it with scissors to prevent it from 'ballooning-up' in oven.)
4   Cook 8 minutes, half turning dish after 4 minutes. Leave to stand for up to 5 minutes then serve with creamed or fried potatoes and vegetables to taste.

Note: do not deep freeze.

Veal cutlets romana (Serves 4)

Ingredients	Imperial	American
25g butter	1oz	$\frac{1}{8}$ cup
1 small onion	1 small	1 small
4 veal cutlets, beaten until very thin, each 125g	each 4oz	each 4oz
4 x 15ml tbsp tomato juice	4 tbsp	6 tbsp
1 x 5ml level tsp dried oregano	1 level tsp	1$\frac{1}{2}$ level tsp
125g Mozzarella cheese	4oz	4oz
4 x 5ml heaped tsp capers	4 heaped tsp	6 heaped tsp
garlic salt to taste	to taste	to taste

1 Place butter in large but fairly shallow dish. Melt, uncovered, 1 minute. Stir in onion. Cook, uncovered, 4 minutes. Add veal cutlets, making sure they form a single layer over base of dish.

2 Cook, uncovered, 2 minutes. Turn over. Cook, uncovered, further 2 minutes. Sprinkle with tomato juice and oregano. Cut cheese into thin slices and stand on top of veal. Sprinkle with capers and garlic salt.

3 Cover with lid or cling film. (If using film, make 2 slits in it with scissors to prevent it from 'ballooning-up' in oven.) Cook 2-3 minutes or until cheese just begins to melt. Serve straight away with pasta and either a salad or vegetables to taste.

Note: do not deep freeze.

Kidneys in red wine (Serves 4)

Ingredients	Imperial	American
6 lamb's kidneys	6	6
50g butter	2oz	$\frac{1}{4}$ cup
75g onion, finely chopped	3oz	1 medium
25g plain flour	1oz	3 level tbsp
150ml or 1$\frac{1}{2}$dl dry red wine	$\frac{1}{4}$pt	$\frac{5}{8}$ cup
2 brown gravy cubes	2	2
50g mushrooms, trimmed and sliced	2oz	$\frac{5}{8}$ cup
2 x 5ml level tsp tomato purée	2 level tsp	3 level tsp
$\frac{1}{4}$ x 5ml level tsp paprika	$\frac{1}{4}$ level tsp	$\frac{1}{2}$ level tsp
$\frac{1}{4}$ x 5ml level tsp salt	$\frac{1}{4}$ level tsp	$\frac{1}{2}$ level tsp
2 x 15ml level tbsp chopped parsley	2 level tbsp	3 level tbsp

1 Skin kidneys, cut in half then remove cores with a sharp knife. Cut kidneys into very thin slices.

2 Melt half the butter in a glass or pottery dish for 1 minute in the microwave. Add kidneys. Stir well with butter. Cook, uncovered, for 2 minutes. Remove from oven and leave on one side temporarily.

3 Place rest of butter in deepish glass or pottery dish. Melt 1 minute in the microwave. Add onion. Cook, uncovered, 2 minutes. Stir in flour then blend in wine. Cook for 3 minutes, stirring briskly at the end of every minute. Crumble in gravy cubes then add mushrooms, tomato purée, paprika, salt and the kidneys, together with the butter in which they were cooked.

4 Cover dish with lid or cling film. (If using film, make 2 slits in it with scissors to prevent it from 'ballooning-up' in oven.) Cook 5 minutes, half turning dish after 2$\frac{1}{2}$ minutes.

5 Serve on a bed of rice and sprinkle with parsley.

Note: this dish is suitable for deep freezing.

Buffet gammon (Serves 10 to 12)

Choose a piece of gammon weighing about 3kg (just over 6lb). Place in large saucepan and cover with cold water. Cook conventionally until water boils. Drain. Repeat once more to remove excessive saltiness. Weigh joint and allow 8 minutes per $\frac{1}{2}$kg (1lb) in the microwave. Stand gammon in a large and fairly shallow glass or pottery dish. (If your oven has a glass tray, stand gammon directly on it.) Should the joint be narrower to one end, cover the narrow part with foil to prevent overcooking. Cover gammon with kitchen paper. Cook for half the total cooking time. Leave to stand 30 minutes. Remove foil, turn gammon over and cover with more kitchen paper. Complete cooking. Leave to rest for a further 30 minutes. Strip off skin, score fat into diamonds then sprinkle with browned crumbs. To decorate, stud diamonds with cloves and cocktail cherries speared on to cocktail sticks.

Note: leftovers may be deep frozen.

Fricassée of chicken (Serves 6)

Ingredients	Imperial	American
1¼kg oven-ready chicken, defrosted if frozen	3lb	48oz
1 medium onion, peeled	1 medium	1 medium
2 large celery stalks	2 large	2 large
1 bag bouquet garni	1 bag	1 bag
2 thick slices fresh lemon	2 thick slices	2 thick slices
2 x 5ml level tsp salt	2 level tsp	3 level tsp
275ml or 3dl water	½pt	1¼ cups
125ml or 1¼dl single or coffee cream	¼pt	⅝ cup
40g butter	1½oz	3 tbsp
40g plain flour	1½oz	4½ level tbsp
2 x 15ml tbsp fresh lemon juice	2 tbsp	3 tbsp
salt and white pepper to taste	to taste	to taste
parsley sprigs for garnishing	for garnishing	for garnishing

1   Divide chicken into small joints. Stand, in single layer, in large but fairly shallow dish. Cut onion into 8 wedges. Break each celery stalk into 4 pieces. Place around chicken. Add bouquet garni then top with lemon slices. Sprinkle with salt. Add water.

2   Cover with lid or cling film. (If using film, cut 2 slits in it with scissors to prevent it from 'ballooning-up' in oven.) Cook ¼ hour, half turning dish after 7½ minutes.

3   Remove dish from microwave. Take out chicken and cut meat into bite-size pieces, discarding skin and bones. Strain liquid and reserve 275ml or 3dl (½pt or 1¼ American cups). Combine with cream.

4   Place butter in large but fairly shallow dish. Melt, uncovered, 1½ minutes. Stir in flour. Very gradually whisk in chicken stock and cream mixture. Return to microwave and cook 5 to 6 minutes or until thick and bubbling, stirring or whisking *after every minute*.

5   Add lemon juice and chicken pieces, stirring thoroughly to mix. Season to taste. Cover dish with lid or cling film (making slits in film as before).

6   Reheat 5 minutes, half turning dish after 2½ minutes. Uncover, garnish with parsley and rolls of grilled bacon. Accompany with freshly boiled rice and vegetables to taste.

Notes: any leftover stock can be used as a base for soup, sauces or stews. This dish can be deep frozen.

Chicken curry with coconut (Serves 6)

Ingredients	Imperial	American
1¼kg oven-ready chicken, defrosted if frozen	3lb	48oz
125ml or 1¼dl boiling water	¼pt	⅝ cup
3 x 15ml level tbsp desiccated coconut	3 level tbsp	4½ level tbsp
2 x 15ml tbsp salad oil	2 tbsp	3 tbsp
250g onions	8oz	2 large
2 large garlic cloves	2 large	2 large
2 x 15ml level tbsp tomato purée	2 level tbsp	3 level tbsp
2 x 15ml level tbsp peach chutney	2 level tbsp	3 level tbsp
3 x 15ml level tbsp curry powder	3 level tbsp	4½ level tbsp
1 x 5ml level tsp powdered cinnamon	1 level tsp	1½ level tsp
2 x 5ml level tsp salt	2 level tsp	3 level tsp

1   Divide chicken into small joints. Stand, in single layer, in large but fairly shallow dish. Cover with lid or cling film. (If using film, make 2 slits in it with scissors to prevent it from 'ballooning-up' in oven.) Cook ¼ hour, half turning dish after 7½ minutes.

2   Make curry sauce on conventional cooker. To make coconut milk pour boiling water over coconut. Cover. Leave to stand temporarily. Heat oil in pan. Add finely chopped onions and crushed garlic. Fry until light gold.

3   Stir in tomato purée, chutney, curry powder and cinnamon. Strain coconut and pour liquid into pan. Mix thoroughly with other ingredients. Sprinkle with salt.

4   Uncover chicken. Coat with sauce. Cover with lid or film (making slits in film as before). Cook 20 minutes, half turning dish after 10 minutes. Leave to stand 5 minutes then serve with freshly cooked long grain rice and side dishes (Sambals) of coconut, chutney, sliced lemon, peanuts, yogurt, chopped or sliced onion, sliced cucumber and sliced tomatoes.

Chicken cacciatora (Serves 6)

Ingredients	Imperial	American
1½kg oven-ready chicken, defrosted if frozen	3lb	48oz
2 x 15ml tbsp corn or olive oil	2 tbsp	3 tbsp
125g onion	4oz	1 large
2 large garlic cloves	2 large	2 large
25g plain flour	1oz	3 level tbsp
½kg canned or fresh tomatoes, skinned and chopped	1lb	2 cups
125ml or 1¼dl hot water	¼pt	⅝ cup
1 brown gravy cube	1	1
3 x 15ml tbsp tomato purée	3 level tbsp	4½ level tbsp
125g trimmed and sliced mushrooms	4oz	1 cup
2 x 5ml level tsp salt	2 level tsp	3 level tsp
1 x 5ml level tsp brown sugar	1 level tsp	1½ level tsp
3 x 15ml tbsp Marsala	3 tbsp	4½ tbsp

1   Divide chicken into small joints. Stand, in single layer, in large but fairly shallow dish. Cover with lid or cling film. (If using film, cut 2 slits in it with scissors to prevent it from 'ballooning-up' in oven.) Cook ¼ hour, half turning dish after 7½ minutes.

2   Meanwhile make sauce on conventional cooker. Heat oil in pan. Add chopped onions and crushed garlic. Fry until pale gold. Stir in flour, tomatoes and water. Crumble in gravy cube then add tomato purée, mushrooms, salt, sugar and Marsala.

3   Cook, stirring continuously, until sauce comes to boil and thickens slightly. Cover. Leave over a low heat until chicken is ready.

4   Uncover chicken. Coat with sauce. Cover with lid or film (making slits in film as before). Cook 20 minutes, half turning dish after 10 minutes.

5   Serve with pasta or rice and a mixed salad.

Note: this dish is suitable for deep freezing.

Chicken marengo (Serves 6)

Follow recipe for chicken cacciatora but use 60g mushrooms, and add 12 stoned black olives and 3 x 15ml heaped tablespoons chopped parsley with the brown sugar. Substitute dry white wine for Marsala.

Note: this dish is suitable for deep freezing.

Coq au vin (Serves 6)

Ingredients	Imperial	American
1½kg oven-ready chicken, defrosted if frozen	3lb	48oz
50g butter	2oz	¼ cup
1 large onion, finely chopped	1 large	1 large
1 medium garlic clove, finely chopped	1 medium	1 medium
2 x 15ml level tbsp plain flour	2 level tbsp	3 level tbsp
275ml or 3dl dry red wine	½pt	1¼ cups
1 brown gravy cube	1	1
1 x 5ml level tsp salt	1 level tsp	1½ level tsp
12 shallots or small onions	12	12
4 x 15ml level tbsp chopped parsley	4 level tbsp	6 level tbsp
1 bag bouquet garni	1 bag	1 bag

1   Divide chicken into 6 joints. Place butter in large but fairly shallow dish. Melt, uncovered, 2 to 3 minutes. Add chicken. Toss over and over in butter. Arrange in dish in single layer.

2   Cover dish with lid or cling film. (If using film, cut 2 slits in it with scissors to prevent it from 'ballooning-up' in oven.) Cook ¼ hour, giving dish a half turn after 7½ minutes.

3   Uncover dish. Sprinkle chicken with onion and garlic. In small basin or jug, gradually mix flour to a smooth liquid with the wine. Whisk if necessary to remove small lumps. Crumble in stock cube then add salt.

4   Pour wine mixture into dish over chicken. Surround with peeled shallots or onions. Sprinkle with parsley then add bouquet garni.

5   Cover dish with lid or film (making slits as before) and cook 20 minutes, half turning dish after 10 minutes. Leave to rest between 5 and 10 minutes then serve with boiled potatoes and a salad or green vegetables to taste.

Note: this dish is suitable for deep freezing.

Chicken in creamed goulash sauce (Serves 6)

Ingredients	Imperial	American
1½kg oven-ready chicken, defrosted if frozen	3lb	48oz
1 large onion	1 large	1 large
1 medium green pepper	1 medium	1 medium
1 medium garlic clove	1 medium	1 medium
2 x 15ml tbsp salad oil	2 tbsp	3 tbsp
40g plain flour	1½oz	6 level tbsp
1 x 15ml level tbsp paprika	1 level tbsp	1½ level tbsp
275ml or 3dl chicken stock	½pt	1¼ cups
2 x 15ml level tbsp tomato purée	2 level tbsp	3 level tbsp
1 x 5ml tsp granulated sugar	1 level tsp	1½ level tsp
½ x 5ml tsp caraway seeds	½ level tsp	¾ level tsp
1 x 5ml level tsp salt	1 level tsp	1½ level tsp
125ml or 1½dl soured cream	¼pt	⅝ cup

1 Divide chicken into 6 joints. Stand, in single layer, in large but fairly shallow dish. Cover with lid or cling film. (If using film, cut 2 slits in it with scissors to prevent it from 'ballooning-up' in oven.) Cook ¼ hour, giving dish a half turn after 7½ minutes.

2 Meanwhile prepare sauce. Finely chop onion, de-seeded green pepper and garlic. Fry conventionally in the oil until golden. Stir in flour and paprika. Gradually blend in stock, tomato purée, sugar, caraway seeds and salt.

3 Cook, stirring, until sauce comes to boil and thickens. Cover and leave until chicken is ready.

4 Uncover chicken and pour juices from dish into sauce. Mix thoroughly. Pour over chicken. Coat with spoons of soured cream.

5 Cover dish with lid or film (making slits in film as before) and cook 20 minutes, half turning dish after 10 minutes. Leave to rest between 5 and 10 minutes then serve with pasta and a green salad.

Note: this dish is suitable for deep freezing.

Country captain (Serves 6)

Ingredients	Imperial	American
50g butter	2oz	¼ cup
175g onions	6oz	2 medium
1¾kg chicken joints	3½lb	3½lb
1 x 15ml level tbsp flour	1 level tbsp	1½ level tbsp
1 x 15ml level tbsp curry powder	1 level tbsp	1½ level tbsp
45g blanched and halved almonds	2½oz	⅓ cup
50g green pepper, de-seeded	2oz	½ medium-sized pepper
3 x 15ml level tbsp sultanas	3 level tbsp	4½ level tbsp
397g canned tomatoes	14oz	1¾ cups
2 x 5ml level tsp celery salt	2 level tsp	3 level tsp
1 x 5ml level tsp salt	1 level tsp	1½ level tsp

1 Place butter in large, but fairly shallow, glass or pottery dish. Melt 2 minutes in microwave.

2 Add finely chopped onions. Cook, uncovered, 2 minutes in microwave. Add chicken joints. Toss over and over in butter/onion mixture so that pieces are well-coated.

3 Sprinkle with flour, curry powder, almonds, finely chopped green pepper and sultanas. Cover dish with lid or cling film. (If using film, make 2 slits in it with scissors to prevent it from 'ballooning-up' in oven.) Cook 15 minutes, half turning dish after 7½ minutes.

4 Take out of oven and leave to stand 5 minutes. Meanwhile, crush tomatoes and combine with celery and ordinary salt. Spoon over chicken in dish. Cover (making 2 slits in film as before). Cook 20 minutes, half turning dish after 10 minutes. Serve with rice.

Notes: this dish is suitable for deep freezing.
Country captain comes from the southern states of the USA and is said to be Anglo-Indian in origin.

Scandinavian risotto   Rice with onion, green pepper and celery, sultanas, ham and pineapple. (Recipe page 82)

Meat and Poultry   **67**

Spanish-style paella (Serves 6)

Ingredients	Imperial	American
1kg, 6 medium chicken joints	2lb	32oz
2 x 15ml tbsp salad oil	2 tbsp	3 tbsp
250g onions	8oz	2 large
2 large garlic cloves	2 large	2 large
1 medium red pepper	1 medium	1 medium
1 medium green pepper	1 medium	1 medium
250g long grain rice (easy cook)	8oz	1¼ cups
1 x 5ml level tsp saffron strands	1 level tsp	1½ level tsp
125g frozen peas	4oz	1 cup
175g canned or fresh skinned tomatoes	6oz	3 medium
About 250g canned mussels in brine	8oz	1 cup
425ml or 4dl boiling water	¾ pint	1⅝ cup
2 x 5ml level tsp salt	2 level tsp	3 level tsp
12 large peeled scampi	12	12 peeled shrimps
paprika for sprinkling	for sprinkling	for sprinkling

1   Divide chicken into small joints. Stand, in single layer, in a large dish of 2½l capacity (5pt or 12½ American cups). Cover with lid or cling film. (If using film, make 2 slits in it with scissors to prevent it from 'ballooning-up' in oven.)

2   Cook ¼ hour, half turning dish after 7½ minutes. Take chicken out of dish and stand temporarily on a plate. Pour liquid into a jug and reserve. Wash and dry dish.

3   Pour oil into clean dish. Add finely chopped onions and garlic. Cook, uncovered, 4 minutes. De-seed peppers and shred. Add half of each to dish with rice, saffron, peas, chopped tomatoes, half the drained mussels, water, reserved liquid and salt. Stir well to mix.

4   Cover with lid or film (making slits in film as before). Cook 20 minutes, half turning dish after 10 minutes. Leave to rest 10 minutes.

5   Cover rest of pepper strips with boiling water. Leave 5 minutes. Drain. Uncover rice, etc and stir. Top attractively with chicken, pepper strips, remaining mussels and scampi. Sprinkle lightly with paprika.

6   Cover. Cook 12 minutes, half turning dish after 6 minutes. Serve straight away.

Notes: in view of the high price of saffron, use if preferred 2 x 5ml level teaspoons (2 level teaspoons or American 3 level teaspoons) turmeric powder which will give the rice its typical yellow colour. Add it at the same time as the water, etc.

This dish is not recommended for deep freezing.

Chicken jumble (Serves 6)

Ingredients	Imperial	American
1½kg chicken joints	3lb	48oz
1 x 5ml level tsp dried tarragon	1 level tsp	1½ level tsp
2 medium garlic cloves	2 medium	2 medium
about 350g sweetcorn kernels	12oz	2 cups
about 275g condensed cream of tomato soup	10oz	10oz

1   Stand chicken joints in large but fairly shallow glass or pottery dish. Sprinkle with tarragon and crushed garlic cloves.

2   Cover with lid or cling film. (If using film, make 2 slits in it with scissors to prevent it from 'ballooning-up' in oven.) Cook ¼ hour, half turning dish after 7½ minutes.

3   Uncover. Add drained sweetcorn. Spread tomato soup over top. Cover with lid or film (making slits in film as before). Cook 20 minutes, half turning dish after 10 minutes. Serve with creamed potatoes and green vegetables to taste.

Note: this dish is suitable for deep freezing.

Turkey español (Serves 4)

Ingredients	Imperial	American
50g butter	2oz	¼ cup
½kg 4 raw turkey breast steaks	1lb	1lb
125g onion	4oz	1 large
12 Spanish stuffed olives	12	12
2 x grade 3 hard-boiled eggs	2 standard	2 medium hard-cooked
2 x 15ml level tbsp chopped gherkins	2 level tbsp	3 level tbsp
1 large tomato	1 large	1 large

1   Place butter in large but fairly shallow glass or pottery dish. Melt 2 minutes in microwave.

2   Add turkey steaks and toss well in the butter, making sure both sides are evenly coated.

3   Finely grate onion. Chop olives and eggs. Combine these three ingredients with the gherkins. Pile equal amounts over turkey steaks. Garnish with sliced tomato.

4   Cover with lid or cling film. (If using film, make 2 slits in it with scissors to prevent it from 'ballooning-

up' in oven.) Cook 10 minutes, half turning dish after 5 minutes.

5   Serve with new potatoes tossed in butter and French beans or leaf spinach. Coat with juices from dish.

Notes: if using frozen turkey, thaw out before cooking. Do not freeze after cooking.

Roast duckling with sage and onion stuffing (Serves 4)

Ingredients	Imperial	American
just over 2kg oven-ready duckling, thawed if frozen	4½lb	4½lb
25g butter or margarine	1oz	⅛ cup
1 packet sage and onion stuffing, about 100g	3½oz	1 cup
275ml or 3dl boiling water	½pt	1¼ cups
salt for sprinkling	for sprinkling	for sprinkling

1   Wash duckling inside and out under cold running water. Wipe dry with paper towels.

2   Place butter or margarine in glass or pottery dish. Melt 1 minute in microwave. Add stuffing mix and water. Stir well. Cook, uncovered, 1 minute in microwave.

3   Leave to cool off slightly then pack into crop end and body cavity of bird.

4   Stand 2 inverted saucers in a large glass or pottery dish (the saucers are used instead of a rack). Place duckling on top, breast side down.

5   Cover completely with cling film, making 2 slits in it with scissors to prevent it from 'ballooning-up' in oven. Cook 22 minutes.

6   Remove dish from oven. Take off cling film. Turn duckling over. Sprinkle breast heavily with salt. Return to microwave.

7   Cook, uncovered, for 23 minutes. Half turn dish after ¼ hour. Leave to rest 10 minutes after cooking. Accompany with thin gravy, apple sauce, potatoes and peas.

Notes: for home-made stuffing, see following recipe. Duckling leftovers may be frozen, but stuffing should be separated from bird first.

Sage and onion stuffing (Sufficient for average size bird or joint of pork)

Ingredients	Imperial	American
$\frac{1}{2}$kg onions	1lb	4 medium
50g butter	2oz	$\frac{1}{4}$ cup
2 x 5ml level tsp dried sage	2 level tsp	3 level tsp
125g fresh white breadcrumbs	4oz	2 cups
salt and pepper to taste	to taste	to taste
1 x grade 3 egg	1 standard	1 medium

1 Peel and very finely grate onion. Melt butter in microwave 1 to $1\frac{1}{2}$ minutes. Add onions. Stir round in butter. Cook, uncovered, 3 to 4 minutes.
2 Add sage, crumbs and seasoning. Toss well to mix. Bind with well beaten egg. Use as required.

Note: this stuffing may be deep frozen for up to about 2 weeks.

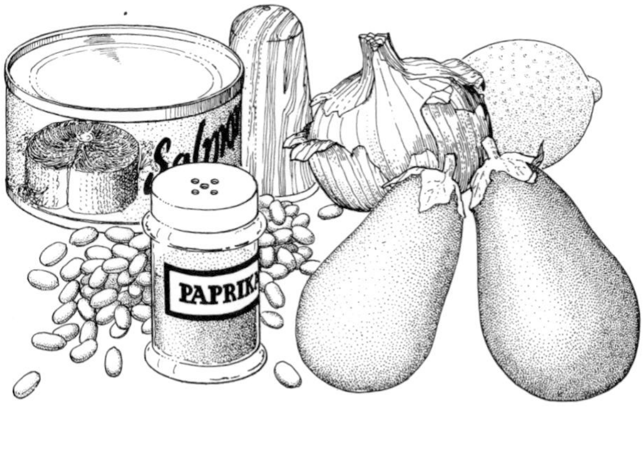

Normandy duck (Serves 4)

Ingredients	Imperial	American
$1\frac{3}{4}$kg duckling joints	$3\frac{1}{2}$lb	$3\frac{1}{2}$lb
1 x 5ml level tsp salt	1 level tsp	$1\frac{1}{2}$ level tsp
2 medium garlic cloves	2 medium	2 medium
12 pitted prunes	12 pitted	12 pitted
3 x 15ml tbsp plain flour	3 level tbsp	$4\frac{1}{2}$ level tbsp
425ml or 4dl dry cider	$\frac{3}{4}$pt	$1\frac{1}{2}$ cups
$\frac{1}{2}$ x 5ml level tsp celery salt	$\frac{1}{2}$ level tsp	$\frac{3}{4}$ level tsp
1 x 5ml level tsp salt	1 level tsp	$1\frac{1}{2}$ level tsp
2 x 5ml level tsp tomato purée	2 level tsp	3 level tsp
2 x 15ml tbsp double cream	2 tbsp	3 tbsp
$\frac{1}{4}$ x 5ml level tsp white pepper	$\frac{1}{4}$ level tsp	$\frac{1}{2}$ level tsp

1 Arrange duckling joints, skin side uppermost, in a large but fairly shallow glass or pottery dish. Sprinkle with salt. Add cut up garlic cloves and prunes.
2 Cover with lid or cling film. (If using film, make 2 slits in it with scissors to prevent it from 'ballooning-up' in oven.) Cook 25 minutes, half turning dish after 12 minutes.
3 Uncover. Pour off fat but reserve 2 tablespoons. Cover duckling in dish with foil to hold in the heat. Place duckling fat in clean dish. Stir in flour. Gradually blend in cider. Cook 5 minutes until thickened, stirring sauce after every minute for smoothness.
4 Remove from microwave. Stir in all remaining ingredients. Pour over duckling in dish. Cook, uncovered, 4 minutes. Half turn dish after 2 minutes.
5 Serve with boiled potatoes and either a salad or green vegetable to taste.

Note: this dish is suitable for freezing.

6 Vegetables

Ratatouille Aubergines, courgettes, green peppers and tomatoes are the basic ingredients—their flavours perfectly preserved. (Recipe page 77)

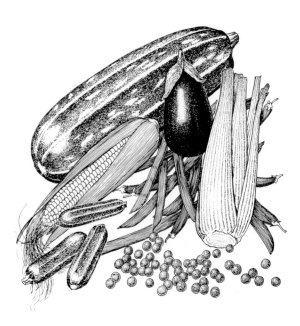

All vegetables have an excellent texture and colour when cooked in a microwave oven and take on a deliciously fresh flavour. A few vegetable dishes have been included in this section but for cooking fresh and frozen vegetables in general, please refer to the following charts.

Cooking fresh vegetables

The use of roasting bags is recommended when cooking fresh vegetables in the microwave oven. The reason for this is that little or no water need be added and therefore the vegetables cook in their own juices. This means that the flavour, colour and nutritive value are retained. Points to remember:

1 Less seasoning is required.

2 The top of the bag should be tied *loosely* with an elastic band, a piece of string or plastic ring to allow the steam to escape.

3 Set the bag on its side (not standing upright) in a dish and place in the oven.

4 Times are approximate as the age and thickness of the vegetables will affect the cooking time. Therefore test regularly during cooking.

5 The times given are for the quantity stated. If the quantity is altered, the time should be adjusted accordingly.

6 Do not overcook as the vegetables will continue to cook for a short while after removal from the oven.

7 Since vegetables will remain hot for a considerable time if the bag is not opened, it is possible to cook several types, one after another, and serve them together.

8 If using a dish, place vegetables inside and cover with lid or cling film. (If using film, make 2 slits in it with scissors to prevent it from 'ballooning-up' in oven.) Add an extra 2 to 3 minutes cooking time to that given on the chart. Remember to add 2 x 15ml tablespoons (2 tablespoons or American 3 tablespoons) water and a light sprinkling of salt. Drain after cooking. Toss with butter.

Note: if using a dish, turn twice or three times during cooking. Alternatively, stir once or twice.

Times for cooking in roasting bags

Vegetable (prepared weight)	Metric and American	Preparation	Quantity of water	Cooking time
8 oz Asparagus medium to thin spears thick spears	225g 8oz	Leave whole, trim	2 x 15ml tablespoons (2 tablespoons or 3 American)	8 minutes 10 minutes
1lb Aubergines	½kg 1lb	Prepare and slice	2 x 15ml tablespoons (2 tablespoons or 3 American)	10 minutes
1lb Beetroot	½kg 1lb	Peel	Cover with cold water. Add no salt.	20 to 25 minutes
3 to 4 Broccoli spears	3 to 4 spears	Split lengthwise if thick	4 x 15ml tablespoons (4 tablespoons or 6 American)	9 to 10 minutes
½lb Brussels sprouts	250g ½lb	Trim	2 x 15ml tablespoons (2 tablespoons or 3 American)	8 to 9 minutes
1lb Cabbage	½kg about 4 to 6 cups	Prepare and shred	2 x 15ml tablespoons (2 tablespoons or 3 American)	10 minutes
8oz Carrots—new	225g 8oz	Scrape, leave whole	2 x 15ml tablespoons (2 tablespoons or 3 American)	10 minutes
8oz Carrots—old	225g 8oz	Scrape and slice	2 x 15ml tablespoons (2 tablespoons or 3 American)	10 minutes
1½lb Cauliflower	¾kg 1½lb	Prepare and cut into flowerets	4 x 15ml tablespoons (4 tablespoons or 6 American)	12 minutes
12oz Celery	350g 12oz	Slice	2 x 15ml tablespoons (2 tablespoons or 3 American)	9 to 10 minutes
2 Corn-on-the-cob	2 medium 2 medium	Remove husks and silk	No water. Add knob of butter	4 to 5 minutes
1lb Courgettes	½kg 1lb	Trim, slice and sprinkle with salt	None	14 minutes
1lb Leeks	½kg 1lb	Trim and slice	2 x 15ml tablespoons (2 tablespoons or 3 American)	10 minutes

Vegetable (prepared weight)	Metric and American	Preparation	Quantity of water	Cooking time
1lb Marrow	½kg 1lb	Small dice	None	12 to 14 minutes
8oz Mushrooms	225g 8oz	Peel or wash	2 x 15ml tablespoons (2 tablespoons or 3 American)	6 minutes
1lb Onions	½kg 1lb	Quarter	None	7 to 8 minutes
1lb Parsnips	½kg 1lb	Peel and dice	2 x 15ml tablespoons (2 tablespoons or 3 American)	10 minutes
1lb Peas	½kg 1lb	Shelled	2 x 15ml tablespoons (2 tablespoons or 3 American)	8 to 9 minutes
1lb Runner beans	½kg 1lb	Prepare and slice	2 x 15ml tablespoons (2 tablespoons or 3 American)	10 minutes
1lb Spinach	½kg 1lb	Prepare, wash and sprinkle with salt	None	8 minutes
1lb Spring greens	½kg 1lb	Prepare, wash and sprinkle with salt	None	8 minutes
1lb Swedes	½kg 1lb	Peel and dice	2 x 15ml tablespoons (2 tablespoons or 3 American)	10 minutes
1lb Turnips	½kg 1lb	Peel and dice	2 x 15ml tablespoons (2 tablespoons or 3 American)	10 minutes

Notes: a small quantity of salt may be added to the bag. Alternatively, season and toss with butter after cooking and draining.

For superbly-flavoured corn-on-the-cob, cook it wrapped in its own husk and silk instead of in a roasting bag or dish. Stand on kitchen paper in the microwave and allow: *1 corn* 2 minutes; *2 corn* 4 to 5 minutes; *3 corn* 6 to 7 minutes; *4 corn* 8 to 10 minutes. After cooking, wrap in foil, leave to stand 5 minutes then strip off husk and silk. Serve with butter and seasonings.

Jacket potatoes stuffed with fried bacon and cheese These potatoes cook with lightning speed in the microwave. (Recipe page 74)

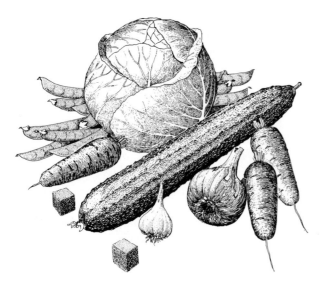

Frozen vegetables

Place vegetables in roasting bag or dish. Add a knob of butter and sprinkling of salt. Tie bag loosely or cover dish. For quantities up to ½kg (1lb), cook for the time recommended on the packet. For larger quantities, increase the cooking time by 1 to 3 minutes, depending on the type of vegetable. If cooking a block of vegetables, place in bag or dish with the ice side uppermost.

If preferred, frozen vegetables may be cooked in their original bag. Snip off one corner, add a little salt and a knob of butter then stand bag in a dish.

Jacket potatoes

These bake with the speed of lightning in the microwave and the texture and flavour are superb. Choose medium-sized and even potatoes of about 125g (4oz) each. Wash well and dry. Prick skins well all over with a fork.

For 1 potato: stand on kitchen paper placed on base of oven. Cook 5 to 6 minutes, turning over once. Leave to stand 5 minutes. Potato will keep hot for about 10 to 15 minutes if wrapped in a cloth.

For 2 potatoes: arrange on paper, leaving 2½cm (1in) space between each potato. Cook 6½ to 8 minutes. *For 3 potatoes:* arrange on paper in shape of triangle, leaving 2½cm (1in) space between each. Cook 9 to 11 minutes. *For 4 potatoes:* arrange on paper in shape of square, leaving 2½cm (1in) space between each. Cook 12 to 14 minutes. *For 5 potatoes:* arrange on paper in shape of ring, leaving 2½cm (1in) space between each. Cook 15 to 17 minutes. *For 6 potatoes:* arrange as for 5 potatoes. Cook 18 to 20 minutes. *For 7 potatoes:* arrange as for 5 potatoes. Cook 20 to 22 minutes. *For 8 potatoes:* arrange as for 5 potatoes. Cook 23 to 25 minutes.

To serve: split in half and top with butter and/or soured cream.

Stuffed jacket potatoes (Allow 2 halves per person)

Halve cooked potatoes. Scoop insides into bowl. Cream with butter or margarine and milk. Season. Add to taste one of the following:
1 Grated cheese, nutmeg, mustard and chopped parsley.
2 Cooked and flaked smoked haddock with chopped egg.
3 Finely chopped fried bacon with grated cheese.
4 Fried onions.
Return mixture to potato shells. Reheat in microwave, allowing 1½ minutes for 2 halves; 2½ minutes for 3 halves; 3 minutes for 4 halves, and so on.

Notes: stuffed potatoes (except those with hard-boiled egg) are suitable for deep freezing.
Cooking and reheating times given are approximate only. Longer or shorter times may be needed according to the model of microwave and size of potatoes. Always undercook slightly rather than overcook. If potatoes feel hard, return to microwave for a further 1 to 3 minutes.

Braised celery (Serves 4)

Ingredients	Imperial	American
350g celery	12oz	12oz
25g butter	1oz	$\frac{1}{8}$ cup
2 medium bacon rashers, chopped	2 medium	2 medium slices or strips
50g onion, chopped	2oz	1 small
275ml or 3dl boiling chicken stock	1pt	1$\frac{1}{4}$ cups bouillon
seasoning to taste	to taste	to taste

1 Cut celery into 5 to 7$\frac{1}{2}$cm (2 to 3in) long strips. Place butter in deepish glass or pottery dish. Melt 1 minute in the microwave. Add celery.
2 Add bacon and onion. Cook, uncovered, for 3 minutes. Pour stock into dish. Season. Cover. Cook 30 minutes, half turning dish after $\frac{1}{4}$ hour. Stir well. Serve hot.

Note: do not freeze.

Courgette casserole (Serves 4)

Ingredients	Imperial	American
225g skinned and chopped tomatoes	8oz	1 cup
225g thinly sliced and unpeeled courgettes	8oz	about 2 cups
125g chopped onion	4oz	about $\frac{3}{4}$ cup
1 x 15ml tbsp vinegar	1 tbsp	1$\frac{1}{2}$ tbsp
2 x 5ml level tsp finely chopped parsley	2 level tsp	3 level tsp
1 garlic clove, crushed	1	1
4 x 15ml level tbsp grated Cheddar cheese	4 level tbsp	6$\frac{1}{2}$ level tbsp

1 Put tomatoes, courgettes, onion, vinegar, parsley and garlic into a glass or pottery dish. Stir well to mix.
2 Cover with cling film, making 2 slits in it with scissors to prevent it from 'ballooning-up' in oven. Cook 14 minutes, half turning dish after 7 minutes.
3 Uncover and sprinkle with cheese. Either brown under a conventional grill or reheat in the microwave for a few minutes or until the cheese melts and becomes bubbly.

Note: this dish is suitable for deep freezing but the cheese should be sprinkled on top after thawing and before reheating.

Cauliflower cheese (Serves 4)

Stand 1 medium trimmed cauliflower upright in a fairly deep glass or pottery dish. Add 4 x 15ml tablespoons (4 tablespoons or American 6 tablespoons) hot water. Cover dish with cling film, making 2 slits in it with scissors to prevent it from 'ballooning-up' in oven. Cook about 11 to 12 minutes, turning dish 4 times. Stand 5 minutes. Drain. Leave cauliflower in same dish. Coat with hot cheese sauce (see Sauces section). Sprinkle with extra grated cheese to taste. Brown in oven or under grill. Alternatively, sprinkle paprika over cheese and return dish to the microwave. Heat a few minutes or until cheese melts.

Note: do not freeze.

Artichokes with hollandaise sauce (Serves 2)

Soak 2 large globe artichokes, leaves down, in a large bowl of cold water for 1 hour. Drain. Stand upright in large glass or pottery dish. Add 1$\frac{1}{4}$cm ($\frac{1}{2}$in) boiling water. Cover with cling film, making 2 slits in it with scissors to prevent it from 'ballooning-up' in oven. Cook $\frac{1}{4}$ hour, half turning dish after 7$\frac{1}{2}$ minutes. Drain and serve hot with hollandaise sauce (see Sauces section).

For 4 artichokes
Stand upright, after soaking, in very large and deep dish. Add 2$\frac{1}{2}$cm (1in) boiling water. Cook 25 minutes.

Notes: if preferred, leave artichokes until cold and serve with French dressing.
Do not deep freeze after cooking.

Stuffed aubergines (Serves 2 as a main course; 4 as a starter)

Ingredients	Imperial	American
½kg 2 aubergines	1lb	1lb eggplants
150g finely grated onion	5oz	1 large
6 x 15ml level tbsp fresh white breadcrumbs	6 level tbsp	9 level tbsp
1 x 5ml level tsp dried marjoram	1 level tsp	1½ level tsp
1 x 5ml level tsp salt	1 level tsp	1½ level tsp
225g tomatoes, skinned and chopped	8oz	3 medium
25g butter	1oz	⅛ cup

1 Wash and dry aubergines. Prick skins all over lightly with a fork. Stand on a plate. Cook, uncovered, 6 minutes in the microwave, half turning plate after 3 minutes.
2 Leave until almost cold then cut aubergines in half lengthwise. Scoop out flesh, taking care not to break aubergine shells. Chop flesh finely and put into bowl. Stir in all remaining ingredients except butter.
3 Stand aubergine shells on a plate and fill with breadcrumb mixture. Melt butter for 1 minute in the microwave.
4 Trickle over aubergines then cook, uncovered, for 6 minutes. Turn plate once or twice during cooking. Stand a few minutes before serving.

Note: do not freeze.

Stuffed peppers (Serves 4)

Ingredients	Imperial	American
½kg 4 medium green peppers	1lb	1lb
25g butter or margarine	1oz	⅛ cup
75g onion	3oz	1 medium
225g lean minced beef	8oz	8oz ground beef
2 x 15ml level tbsp long grain rice	2 level tbsp	3 level tbsp
½ x 5ml level tsp salt	½ level tsp	¾ level tsp
1 x 5ml level tsp mixed herbs	1 level tsp	1½ level tsp
6 x 15ml tbsp hot water	6 tbsp	9 tbsp

1 Cut tops off peppers and remove inside seeds and fibres. If necessary, cut a sliver off the base of each pepper so that it stands upright without toppling.

2 Place butter or margarine in fairly deep glass or pottery dish. Melt 1 minute in microwave. Add finely chopped onion. Cook, uncovered, 3 minutes. Stir in meat. Cook, uncovered, a further 3 minutes.
3 Stir in rice, salt, herbs and 4 tablespoons (American 6 tablespoons) water. Mix thoroughly. Spoon into peppers. Stand upright in clean dish. Add rest of water.
4 Cover dish with cling film, making 2 slits in it with scissors to prevent it from 'ballooning-up' in oven.
5 Cook 15 minutes, half turning dish after 7½ minutes. Leave to stand, covered, for 10 minutes before serving.

Note: this dish is suitable for deep freezing.

Ratatouille (Serves 6)

Ingredients	Imperial	American
50g butter	2oz	¼ cup
2 x 15ml tbsp corn oil	2 tbsp	3 tbsp
175g onion	6oz	1 large
1 large garlic clove	1 large	1 large
225g courgettes, thinly sliced	8oz	2 cups about
350g aubergines, thinly sliced	12oz	2 medium
125g green pepper, finely chopped	4oz	1 cup
225g skinned and chopped tomatoes	8oz	1¼ cups
2 x 15ml level tbsp finely chopped parsley	2 level tbsp	3 level tbsp
2 x 5ml level tsp salt	2 level tsp	3 level tsp

1 Place butter and oil in large glass or pottery dish. Melt 2 minutes in the microwave.
2 Stir in thinly sliced onion and crushed garlic. Cook, uncovered, 5 minutes.
3 Add courgettes, aubergines, green pepper, tomatoes, parsley and half the salt. Stir well to mix. Cover dish with lid or cling film. (If using film, make 2 slits in it with scissors to prevent it from 'ballooning-up' in oven.)
4 Cook 20 minutes, giving dish a quarter turn every 5 minutes. Uncover. Return to microwave and cook, uncovered, a further 5 to 8 minutes or until most of the excess liquid has evaporated. Stir in rest of salt. Serve as an accompaniment to meat and poultry.

Notes: this dish is suitable for deep freezing.
For a meatless main course, serve the ratatouille on top of portions of freshly cooked rice. Sprinkle with grated cheese.

Gratin dauphinoise (Serves 6)

Ingredients	Imperial	American
1kg potatoes, peeled	2lb	32oz
350g mixture of Emmental and Gruyère cheese	12oz	3 cups
freshly milled black pepper to taste	to taste	to taste
275ml or 3dl milk	½pt	1¼ cups
2 x grade 3 eggs	2 standard	2 medium
½ x 5ml level tsp grated nutmeg	½ level tsp	½ level tsp

1 Cut potatoes into wafer-thin slices. Brush a large but fairly shallow dish with melted butter.

2 Fill with layers of potato slices and cheese, beginning and ending with potatoes and seasoning with milled pepper between layers.

3 Cover with lid or cling film. (If using film, cut 2 slits in it with scissors to prevent it from 'ballooning-up in oven.) Cook 20 minutes, half turning dish after 10 minutes. Leave to rest for 5 minutes.

4 Beat milk and eggs lightly together. Pour into dish over potatoes and cheese, lifting mixture with a spoon around edges to enable milk and eggs to reach base of dish. Sprinkle with nutmeg.

5 Cover dish with lid or film (making slits in film as before). Cook ¼ hour, half turning dish after 7½ minutes. Leave to rest 5 minutes before spooning on to warm plates.

Notes: this Swiss classic is nourishing, wholesome and sustaining and makes an unusual and tasty lunch or supper dish. It teams excellently with freshly cooked peas or green beans. Also with a crisp green salad.
It is not suitable for deep freezing and toughens on reheating.

7 Rice and Pasta

As with sauces, I found no advantage initially in cooking rice or pasta in a microwave oven when the conventional cooking time was the same. Then curiosity got the better of me and I tried a few experiments. There was indeed no saving in time except that I could leave the rice or pasta to cook away without much (if any) stirring, there was no boiling over, no steam in the kitchen, no tacky saucepan to wash and, best of all, the pasta was always *al dente*—the correct firm consistency by Italian standards—and never soft and soggy, while the rice grains were always dry, separate and fluffy. I concluded there were advantages to be gained.

American-type long grain or patna (Indian) rice

Place 225g (8oz or American 1 cup) rice into a 1½l (2½pt) glass or pottery dish. Add 575ml (1pt or American 2½ cups) *boiling* water with a generous knob of butter or margarine. Stir. Cover. Cook 13 to 15 minutes. Leave to stand 10 to 15 minutes or until all the water has been absorbed. Add salt to taste. Fluff up with a fork. (Serves 4 to 5)

Elbow or broken macaroni, small pasta or noodles

Cook as rice, adding 1 x 5ml level teaspoon (1 level teaspoon or American 1½ level teaspoons) each, salt and salad oil to the pasta and water. Cook, uncovered, 10 to 15 minutes. Cover. Leave to stand about ¼ hour or until pasta has swollen and little water remains. Drain if necessary. (Serves 4 to 5)

Spaghetti

Cook as macaroni but break in half or thirds if very long. Arrange in deepish oblong dish. Add boiling water to cover.

Lasagne   Cheese sauce and bolognese sauce with leaves of lasagne (white here, green if you prefer). (Recipe page 83)

Scandinavian risotto (Serves 4)

Ingredients	Imperial	American
50g butter	2oz	¼ cup
175g onions	6oz	2 medium
125g green pepper	4oz	1 medium
1 large celery stalk	1 large	1 large
225g 'Easy cook' long grain rice	8oz	1¼ cups
575ml or 6dl boiling water	1pt	2½ cups
2 x 15ml level tbsp raisins or sultanas	2 level tbsp	3 level tbsp
225g lean ham, cut into small cubes	8oz	2 cups
4 medium pineapple rings, well drained	4 medium	4 medium

1   Place butter in large and deep glass or pottery dish. Melt 2 minutes in microwave.
2   Finely chop onions. Thinly slice de-seeded green pepper and celery. Add vegetables to dish and stir round in butter. Cook, uncovered, 2 minutes.
3   Stir in rice. Cook, uncovered, a further 2 minutes. Pour in boiling water. Add raisins or sultanas. Stir. Cover dish with lid or cling film. (If using film, make 2 slits in it with scissors to prevent it from 'ballooning up' in oven.)
4   Cook 15 to 20 minutes or until it is obvious that most of the liquid has been absorbed by the rice. Uncover and stir in ham and pineapple. Adjust seasoning to taste, bearing in mind ham may be salty.
5   Cover dish and leave to stand 10 minutes. Serve with a mixed salad.

Note: this dish is suitable for deep freezing.

Macaroni cheese (Serves 4 to 5)

Ingredients	Imperial	American
225g elbow or broken macaroni	8oz	2 cups
575ml or 6dl boiling water	1pt	2½ cups
2 x 5ml tsp salad oil	2 tsp	3 tsp
1 x 5ml level tsp salt	1 level tsp	1½ level tsp
25g butter or margarine	1oz	⅛ cup
2 x 15ml level tbsp cornflour	2 level tbsp	3 level tbsp cornstarch
275ml or 3dl milk	½pt	1¼ cups
75g grated Cheddar cheese	3oz	¾ cup
Topping		
Grated Cheddar cheese	1oz	¼ cup
1 x 5ml level tsp paprika	1 level tsp	1½ level tsp

1   Place macaroni in large and deep glass or pottery dish. Pour in boiling water and oil. Stir in salt. Cook, uncovered, for 8 to 10 minutes in microwave or until macaroni is plump and tender and most of the water has been absorbed. Stir once or twice.
2   Remove from oven. Add butter or margarine. Mix cornflour to smooth cream with a little of the cold milk. Blend in rest of milk. Pour over macaroni. Mix well. Return to microwave. Cook, uncovered, 8 minutes, stirring well after every 2 minutes.
3   Remove from oven. Add cheese and stir until melted. Sprinkle rest of cheese and paprika on top.
4   Cook a further minute, half turning dish after 30 seconds.

Note: this dish is suitable for deep freezing.

Italian risotto (Serves 4 as a main course; 8 as a starter)

Ingredients	Imperial	American
25g butter	1oz	⅛ cup
3 x 5ml tsp olive oil	3 tsp	4½ tsp
75g onion, chopped	3oz	1 small to medium
150ml or 1½dl dry white wine	¼pt	⅝ cup
350g round grain or Italian rice	12oz	1¾ cups
1¼l boiling chicken stock	2pt	5 cups bouillon
salt and pepper to taste	to taste	to taste
4 x 15ml level tbsp grated Parmesan cheese	4 level tbsp	6 level tbsp

1   Place butter in large glass or pottery dish. Melt 1 minute in the microwave. Add oil and onion. Stir well. Cook, uncovered, 4 minutes.
2   Stir in wine and rice. Cook, uncovered, 5 minutes. Stir 3 to 4 times.
3   Pour in stock. Mix well. Cook, uncovered, 8 minutes or until risotto mixture is thick. Stir every 2 minutes and allow an extra 1 to 2 minutes cooking time if an excessive amount of stock remains.
4   Remove from oven, season well to taste then gently stir in cheese with a fork. Cover. Leave to stand 5 minutes.
5   Serve hot, passing extra grated Parmesan cheese separately.

Note: this dish is suitable for freezing.

Lasagne (Serves 6)

Ingredients	Imperial	American
bolognese sauce—Made up following recipe on page 89.		
425ml or 4dl cheese sauce		
(see page 86)	$\frac{3}{4}$pt	1$\frac{1}{2}$ cups
175g (8 leaves) lasagne	6oz	each 10 x 2in
1l boiling water	1$\frac{3}{4}$pt	4$\frac{3}{8}$ cups
2 x 5ml tsp salad oil	2 tsp	3 tsp
1 x 5ml level tsp salt	1 level tsp	1$\frac{1}{2}$ level tsp
50g grated Cheddar cheese	2oz	$\frac{1}{2}$ cup

1   Make up bolognese and cheese sauces in the microwave and keep hot.
2   To cook lasagne, arrange leaves in an oblong glass or pottery dish about 5cm (2in) in depth. Add water, salad oil and salt. Cook, uncovered, in microwave for 10 minutes. Move gently with a wooden spoon. Cook, uncovered further 5 minutes.
3   Remove from oven, cover with a folded tea-towel and leave to stand 10 minutes. Drain off water and dry lasagne with paper towels.
4   Fill a large oblong dish with alternate layers of cheese sauce, bolognese sauce and lasagne, beginning and ending with the cheese sauce. Sprinkle grated cheese on top.

5   Return to the microwave and cook 10 minutes. Serve hot with a green salad.

Note: this dish is suitable for freezing.

Lasagne verdi (Serves 6)

Make as above, using green lasagne instead of white.

8 Sauces

When you compare the time it takes to make an ordinary white sauce conventionally and then in a microwave oven, you will see there is very little difference and may well ask yourself whether it is worth the bother as I did at first. But I found that the smoothness of a sauce was easier to control in a microwave, there were no messy pans to clean up afterwards and chopped-up meat or poultry could be added directly to the dish. After which it could be reheated quickly and taken straight to the table. It was worthwhile.

The hollandaise and béarnaise sauces never fail—yet they are two of the most tricky to make—the creaminess and flavour of the bread sauce is a joy, the apple sauce has a fresh and fruity tang, and the hot chocolate and mocha marshmallow sauces are speedy to make and work like a charm.

Meat or poultry gravy (Serves 6)

Reserve 2 x 15ml tablespoons (2 tablespoons or American 3 tablespoons) fat from 'roasting' meat or poultry in the microwave. Put into fairly deep glass or pottery dish. Stir in 1 x 15ml level tablespoon (1 level tablespoon or American $1\frac{1}{2}$ level tablespoons) cornflour (American cornstarch). Crumble in 1 brown gravy cube or add 1 x 5ml level teaspoon (1 level teaspoon or American $1\frac{1}{2}$ level teaspoons) brown gravy powder. Gradually blend in 275ml or 3dl ($\frac{1}{2}$pt or American $1\frac{1}{4}$ cups) cold water. Cook 4 to 5 minutes, uncovered, in the microwave. Stir briskly at the end of every minute. Season to taste with salt and pepper. Use as required.

For a thicker gravy: use double amount of cornflour (cornstarch).

For a special occasion gravy: add dry sherry to taste.

Note: gravy is suitable for deep freezing.

Basting sauce (For brushing over poultry and meat)

Melt 25g (1oz or American $\frac{1}{8}$ cup) butter for 1 minute in the microwave. Stir in 1 x 5ml level teaspoon (1 tea-

Hollandaise sauce   Easy to keep to a perfect consistency if you watch your cooking times carefully. (Receipe page 87)

spoon or American 1½ teaspoons) paprika and the same amount of soy sauce. If liked, add a small amount of garlic or onion powder (not salt) for increased flavour. Brush over poultry and joints of meat before cooking in the microwave.

Bread sauce (For poultry)

Ingredients	Imperial	American
125g onion	4oz	1 medium
4 cloves	4	4
275ml or 3dl milk	½pt	1¼ cups
¼ x 5ml level tsp grated nutmeg	¼ level tsp	2 large pinches
65g fresh white breadcrumbs (no crusts)	2½oz	1¼ cups loosely packed
15g butter	½oz	1 tbsp
1 x 15ml tbsp whipping cream	1 tbsp	1½ tbsp

1 Peel onion and press cloves into flesh. Place in deepish glass or pottery dish. Add milk and nutmeg. Cook in microwave, uncovered, for 4 minutes.

2 Stir in breadcrumbs. Cook, uncovered, 2 minutes. Remove onion. Add butter and cream to sauce and mix well. Return to microwave. Cook 30 seconds. Stir. Cook a further 30 seconds. Stir.

3 Adjust seasoning to taste and serve hot.

Note: the sauce is suitable for deep freezing.

Basic white sauce (Serves 4)

Ingredients	Imperial	American
25g butter or margarine	1oz	⅛ cup
25g plain flour	1oz	3 level tbsp
275ml or 3dl cold milk	½pt	1¼ cups
salt and pepper to taste	to taste	to taste

1 Place butter or margarine in fairly deep glass or pottery dish. Melt 1 minute in microwave. Remove from oven.

2 Stir in flour. Gradually blend in milk. Return to microwave and cook 5 to 6 minutes or until thickened, whisking well at the end of every minute.

3 Season to taste and use as required.

Variations on basic white sauce

Add the following 2 minutes before the end of cooking time:

Anchovy sauce (Serve with fish dishes)

2 or 3 x 5ml teaspoons (2 or 3 teaspoons or American 3 or 4 teaspoons) anchovy essence and the same amount of lemon juice. Season to taste.

Caper sauce (Serve with lamb, skate, herrings and mackerel)

2 x 15ml tablespoons (2 tablespoons or American 3 tablespoons) chopped capers and half the amount of caper vinegar. Season to taste.

Cheese sauce (Serve with bacon, ham, poultry, fish, vegetables and hard-boiled eggs)

75g (3oz or American ¾ cup) grated Cheddar cheese and 1 x 5ml teaspoon prepared mustard.

Egg sauce (Serve with poached, steamed or grilled fish dishes and roast poultry)

2 chopped hard-boiled (American hard-cooked) eggs. Season to taste.

Mushroom sauce (Serve with fish, light meats, poultry and vegetables)

4 x 15ml heaped tablespoons (4 heaped tablespoons or American 6 heaped tablespoons) thinly sliced and butter-fried mushrooms. Season to taste.

Mustard sauce (Serve with ham, bacon, tongue, herring, mackerel and cheese dishes)

3 x 5ml level teaspoons (3 level teaspoons or American 4½ level teaspoons) prepared mustard. Season to taste.

Onion sauce (Serve with lamb, tripe and boiled bacon)

2 medium boiled and finely chopped onions and nutmeg to taste. Season.

Parsley sauce (Serve with fish dishes, lamb, ham and boiled bacon)

4 x 15ml level tablespoons (4 level tablespoons or American 6 level tablespoons) finely chopped parsley. Season to taste.

Prawn sauce (Serve with fish dishes)

6 x 15ml level tablespoons (6 level tablespoons or American 9 level tablespoons) peeled prawns (American shrimp). Season to taste with salt, pepper, Worcester sauce, lemon juice and prepared mustard.

Basic pouring sauce

For a sauce with a thinner consistency, follow basic white sauce recipe, halving the amounts of fat and flour.

Note: all these sauces are suitable for deep freezing.

Hollandaise sauce (Serves 4)

Ingredients	Imperial	American
125g butter (slightly salted)	4oz	½ cup
strained lemon juice of		
1 medium lemon	1 medium lemon	1 medium lemon
2 egg yolks	2	2

1   Place butter in glass or pottery jug. Melt 2 minutes in microwave.
2   Add lemon juice and egg yolks. Whisk well to combine ingredients.
3   Return to microwave. Cook, uncovered, 45 seconds. Remove from oven, whisk briefly and adjust seasoning to taste. Serve with hot globe artichokes, or over poached salmon, cauliflower or broccoli.

Notes: this sauce has a perfect consistency and compared with the traditional method is incredibly quick and easy to make. All the same, cooking times are critical and, if you have a high-powered oven, cook for 30 seconds instead of 45. If your oven is slow, you may need to increase cooking time by 15 seconds. The sauce is sufficiently cooked when it is thick enough to coat the back of a spoon.

Leftover sauce should be covered and refrigerated. Reheat by warming 30–40 seconds in the microwave. Whisk and serve.
Do not freeze.

Béarnaise sauce (Serves 4)

This classic sauce for steak and poached eggs is made in the same way as hollandaise with a slight ingredient variation. Omit lemon juice altogether. Instead, place 2 x 15ml tablespoons (2 tablespoons or American 3 tablespoons) white vinegar into dish. Add 1 small peeled and chopped onion, 1 level teaspoon dried tarragon and one or two grindings of coarsely milled black pepper. Cook, uncovered, 4 minutes. Strain. Continue as directed for hollandaise sauce, using strained vinegar in place of lemon.

Note: do not freeze.

Apple sauce (Serves 6)

Ingredients	Imperial	American
½kg cooking apples	1lb	1lb
2 x 15ml tbsp water	2 tbsp	3 tbsp
2 x 5ml level tsp castor sugar	2 level tsp	3 level tsp
Salt and white pepper to taste	to taste	to taste

1   Peel and core apples. Slice thinly into glass or pottery dish. Add water. Cover dish with lid or cling film. (If using film, make 2 slits in it with scissors to prevent it from 'ballooning-up' in oven.)
2   Cook 8 minutes, giving dish a quarter turn every 2 minutes. Remove from oven. Take off film. Beat apples until smooth and pulpy. Stir in sugar. Season to taste with salt and pepper.
3   Serve lukewarm or cold with roast duck, goose or pork.

Notes: for a purée-type sauce, place cooked apples, sugar and seasoning into liquidiser goblet and blend until smooth.
For increased flavour, add 2 or 3 cloves to apples while they are cooking.
The sauce is suitable for deep freezing.

Hot chocolate fudge sauce **Delicious with profiteroles, ice cream, sundaes and many other puddings and desserts. (Recipe page 89)**

Spaghetti bolognese sauce (Serves 6)

Ingredients	Imperial	American
½kg minced beef, lean	1lb	16oz
1 medium onion	1 medium	1 medium
1 large garlic clove	1 large	1 large
1 medium green pepper	1 medium	1 medium
½kg size canned tomatoes	1lb	2 cups
2 x 15ml level tbsp tomato purée	2 level tbsp	3 level tbsp
1 brown gravy cube	1	1
2 x 5ml tsp Worcester sauce	2 tsp	3 tsp
2 x 5ml level tsp dried basil or oregano	2 level tsp	3 level tsp
1 x 5ml level tsp salt	1 level tsp	1½ level tsp

1 Place mince in large but fairly shallow dish. Finely grate onion. Chop garlic. Finely chop de-seeded green pepper. Add onion, garlic and pepper to mince. Fork-mix thoroughly. Cook, uncovered, 5 minutes.
2 Crush canned tomatoes with spoon and add to mince, etc with tomato purée. Crumble gravy cube over the top then add Worcester sauce, basil or oregano and salt. Stir well to mix.
3 Cover with lid or cling film. (If using film, make 2 slits in it with scissors to prevent it from 'ballooning-up' in oven.) Cook ¼ hour, half turning dish after 7½ minutes.
4 Leave to rest 5 minutes, stir round, then serve with freshly cooked spaghetti or other pasta.

Hot chocolate fudge sauce (Serves 6 to 8)

Ingredients	Imperial	American
25g butter	1oz	⅛ cup
75g soft brown sugar	3oz	⅜ cup
2 x 15ml level tbsp cocoa powder, sifted	2 level tbsp	3 level tbsp
2 x 15ml level tbsp cold milk	2 level tbsp	3 level tbsp
1 x 5ml level tsp vanilla essence	1 level tsp	1½ level tsp vanilla extract

1 Melt butter in microwave 1 minute.
2 Stir in all remaining ingredients. Cook, uncovered, 2 minutes. Stir well and spoon over ice cream or ice cream sundaes.

Notes: the sauce is very good served hot with baked sponge-type puddings or allowed to cool and then spooned over profiteroles.
Do not freeze.

Mocha marshmallow sauce (Serves 8)

Ingredients	Imperial	American
125g butter	4oz	½ cup
75g soft brown sugar	3oz	⅜ cup
125g marshmallows	4oz	4oz
2 x 15ml tbsp whipping cream	2 tbsp	3 tbsp
1 x 5ml tsp vanilla essence	1 tsp	1½ tsp vanilla extract
2 x 5ml level tsp instant coffee powder	2 level tsp	3 level tsp

1 Place butter in deep dish and melt for 2 minutes in the microwave.
2 Stir in all remaining ingredients. Cook, uncovered, 1 minute. Stir thoroughly. Repeat once more. Return sauce to microwave and cook a further ½ minute.
3 Stir thoroughly and use as required.

Notes: this is an excellent sauce for sponge-type puddings and cakes as well as ice cream and ice cream sundaes.
Do not freeze.

9 Puddings

All the old favourites are here and all are delicious by virtue of texture and flavour. If you gave up making suet puddings a long time ago because of the length of time they took to steam; if you abandoned egg custards totally because they separated out; if your jam puddings were too costly on fuel and therefore a thing of the past; if you dreaded making mousse because the gelatine went lumpy and the chocolate grainy—well, you can revise your thinking and try your hand at some of these. Follow the recipes closely and you should have no problems; and what a bonus to be able to produce on-the-spot Christmas puddings! As some of the recipes in this section are akin to those in the Cakes section, I suggest you read the introduction to that section as a useful guide.

Defrosting frozen fruit

Remove fruit from packet and stand in dish. Cover with inverted plate to prevent spluttering. Allow:
1 Small fruit such as raspberries and strawberries: 2 to $2\frac{1}{2}$ minutes for every 275g (10oz) pack.
2 Chunky fruits such as peaches and melon balls in syrup: 3 to $3\frac{1}{2}$ minutes for every 275g (10oz) pack.

If fruit is in a plastic bag, puncture 2 or 3 times and stand in a dish. Heat as directed above. A cover is unnecessary.

Fresh fruit cooking chart

Most fruits can be prepared, sprinkled with sugar and cooked in a roasting bag in a similar manner to fresh vegetables (see page 70). The fruit should be checked regularly to make sure that it is not over-cooked. Alternatively, a covered casserole may be used, but as it is necessary to add liquid, the cooking time should be increased by 1 or 2 minutes. Hot water speeds cooking and about 2 to 3 x 15ml tablespoons (2 to 3 tablespoons or 3 to $4\frac{1}{2}$ tablespoons American) should be added to every $\frac{1}{2}$kg (1 lb) prepared fruit.

Fruit	Metric and American	Preparation	Cooking time
1lb Apricots	½kg 1lb	Stone and wash, sprinkle with 125g (4oz) sugar	6 to 8 minutes
1lb Cooking apples	½kg 1lb	Peel, core and slice, sprinkle with 125g (4oz) sugar	8 minutes
1lb Gooseberries	½kg 1lb	Top and tail, sprinkle with 125g (4oz) sugar	4 minutes
4 medium Peaches	4 medium 4 medium	Stone and wash, sprinkle with 125g (4oz) sugar	4 minutes
6 medium Pears	6 medium 6 medium	Peel, halve and core. Dissolve 75g (3oz) sugar and a pinch of cinnamon in a little hot water	8 to 10 minutes
1lb Plums	½kg 1lb	Stone and wash, sprinkle with 125g (4oz) sugar. Add grated rind of ½ lemon	4 minutes
1lb Rhubarb	½kg 1lb	Trim, wash and cut into small pieces, sprinkle with 125g (4oz) sugar and grated peel of 1 lemon	10 minutes

Apricot and almond upside-down orange pudding
(Serves 8)

Ingredients	Imperial	American
50g butter	2oz	¼ cup
50g soft brown sugar	2oz	¼ cup
439g canned apricots	15½oz	2 cups
50g toasted almond nibs	2oz	½ cup
225g self-raising flour	8oz	2 cups
125g butter or margarine	4oz	½ cup
125g castor sugar	4oz	½ cup
finely grated peel of 1 medium orange	1 medium orange	1 medium orange
2 x grade 3 eggs	2 standard	2 medium
5 x 15ml tbsp milk	5 tbsp	7½ tbsp

1 Well butter a dish measuring 30 x 18¾cm (12 x 7½in). Add butter. Melt 2 minutes in the microwave. Sprinkle brown sugar over butter, almost completely covering base of dish.

2 Drain apricots, reserving syrup. Arrange apricots in 4 rows over base of dish, leaving spaces between rows. Fill spaces with almond nibs.

3 Sift flour into bowl. Rub in butter or margarine. Toss in sugar and orange peel.

4 Mix to a batter with eggs and milk, stirring briskly without beating. Cook, uncovered, 10 minutes in the microwave. Stand 5 minutes.

5 Invert on to a large flat plate and serve with reserved syrup, warmed through for about 2 minutes in a jug in the microwave.

Note: do not freeze.

Pears in red wine   A classic favourite recipe, here translated for the microwave. (Recipe page 94)

Fresh fruit crumble (Serves 4 to 6)

Ingredients	Imperial	American
½kg prepared weight apples, blackberries, apricots, plums, gooseberries or combination of fruit	1lb prepared weight	3 to 4 cups
75 to 125g castor sugar, depending on fruit	3 to 4oz depending on fruit	⅜ to ½ cup
Crumble topping		
175g plain flour	6oz	¾ cup
125g butter	4oz	½ cup
75g Demerara sugar	3oz	⅜ cup
1 x 5ml level tsp finely grated lemon peel	1 level tsp	1½ level tsp

1   Prepare fruit according to type: slice apples: hull blackberries; stone apricots and plums, top and tail gooseberries. Place in 1l (1¾pt) glass or pottery dish.
2   Sprinkle with sugar. Stir well to mix.
3   To make crumble, sift flour into a bowl. Rub in butter finely. Toss in grated peel and two-thirds of the sugar.
4   Spoon evenly on top of fruit. Sprinkle rest of sugar on top. Cook in microwave 15 minutes, half turning dish after 7½ minutes. Serve hot with cream, custard or ice cream.

Notes: if using unsweetened frozen fruits, thaw completely before cooking.
This dish is suitable for deep freezing.

'Baked' egg custard (Serves 2 to 3)

Ingredients	Imperial	American
3 x grade 3 eggs	3 standard	3 medium
1 egg yolk	1	1
5 x 15ml level tbsp castor sugar	5 level tbsp	7½ level tbsp
½ x 5ml tsp vanilla essence	½ tsp	¾ tsp vanilla extract
275ml or 3dl milk	½pt	1¼ cups
½ x 5ml level tsp grated nutmeg	½ level tsp	¾ level tsp

1   Place eggs, yolk, sugar and vanilla in a 1l (1¾pt) glass or pottery dish. Beat ingredients well to blend.
2   Pour milk into jug and heat, uncovered, 3 minutes in the microwave. Whisk into egg mixture.
3   Place dish of custard in a 2l (3½pt) fairly shallow

glass or pottery dish. Pour boiling water into the large dish until it reaches the level of the custard in the smaller dish.

4   Cook in the microwave for 6 to 8 minutes or until custard is only just set. Take dish of custard out of water bath and serve warm or cold.

Notes: it is advisable to remove custard from the oven when the centre is not completely set. It will set on cooling.

Do not freeze.

Pears in wine (Serves 6)

Ingredients	Imperial	American
425ml or 4dl dry red wine	¾pt	1½ cups
75g castor sugar	3oz	⅜ cup
¾kg dessert pears	1½lb	6 medium
2 x 15ml level tbsp cornflour	2 level tbsp	3 level tbsp cornstarch
5 x 15ml tbsp cold water	5 tbsp	7½ tbsp
1 x 5ml red food colouring	1 tsp	1½ tsp
about 3 x 15ml level tbsp blanched and toasted almonds, cut into slivers	3 level tbsp	4½ level tbsp

1   Place wine and sugar in a fairly large and deep glass or pottery dish. Stir well. Cook, uncovered, in microwave for 3 minutes.

2   Peel pears without removing stalks. Place, on their sides, in wine. Cook, covered, 4 minutes. Turn over. Cook, covered, a further 4 minutes.

3   Carefully lift pears out of wine and stand upright in a fairly shallow serving dish.

4   Mix cornflour to a smooth cream with cold water. Add to wine mixture. Cook in microwave, uncovered, 5 minutes, stirring briskly at the end of every minute. When wine sauce is ready, it should be clear and thickened.

5   Heighten colour, if necessary, with red food colouring. Pour over pears. Spike fruit with almond as shown in photograph. Chill lightly before serving. Accompany with whipped cream.

Note: do not freeze.

Compôte of dried fruit (Serves 4)

Ingredients	Imperial	American
125g dried apricots	4oz	4oz
125g pitted prunes	4oz	4oz
275ml or 3dl boiling water	½pt	1¼ cups
50g castor sugar	2oz	¼ cup
2 x 5ml level tsp coarsely grated lemon peel	2 level tsp	3 level tsp

1   Wash fruit and soak overnight in plenty of water. Drain thoroughly. Place in fairly deep pottery or glass dish.

2   Add boiling water, sugar and lemon peel. Mix well. Cover with lid or cling film. (If using film, make 2 slits in it with scissors to prevent it from 'ballooning-up' in oven.)

3   Cook about ½ hour or until tender, half turning dish after 15 minutes.

4   Serve hot or very cold. Accompany with sponge cake and whipped cream as an optional extra.

Note: this dish is suitable for deep freezing.

'Baked' stuffed apples

This is a rapid operation in the microwave and the apples develop a remarkably fresh and rounded fruity flavour.

For two servings, wash and dry 2 medium-sized cooking apples. Remove cores then score a line round each apple about ⅓ of the way down from the top. Stand in a shallow glass or pottery dish and pack centres with soft brown sugar, sultanas or currants and a little lemon juice. Top each with a small knob of butter and cook, uncovered, for 5 minutes in the microwave.

For 1 apple: cook 3 to 4 minutes. *For 4 apples:* space apples out in dish so that they are towards the outside and not clustered together in the centre. Cook 8 to 10 minutes.

Note: do not freeze.

Semolina pudding (Serves 4)

Ingredients	Imperial	American
50g fine semolina	2oz	$\frac{1}{4}$ cup
25 to 50g castor sugar	1 to 2oz	$\frac{1}{8}$ to $\frac{1}{4}$ cup
575ml or 6dl milk	1pt	$2\frac{1}{2}$ cups
15g butter	$\frac{1}{2}$oz	1 tbsp

1 Place semolina in a deepish glass or pottery dish. Add sugar then blend in milk.
2 Cook, uncovered, in the microwave for 8 minutes, stirring briskly at the end of every minute.
3 Remove from oven, stir in butter. Serve straight away.

Lemon or orange semolina pudding (Serves 4)

Make as above, adding the finely grated peel of half a small washed and dried lemon or orange with the sugar.

Note: do not freeze either of these two puddings.

Steamed syrup suet pudding (Serves 4 to 5)

Ingredients	Imperial	American
3 x 15ml tbsp melted golden syrup	3 tbsp	$4\frac{1}{2}$ tbsp light corn syrup
125g self-raising flour	4oz	1 cup
50g finely shredded suet	2oz	$\frac{1}{2}$ cup
50g castor sugar	2oz	$\frac{1}{4}$ cup
1 x 5ml level tsp vanilla essence	1 level tsp	$1\frac{1}{2}$ level tsp vanilla extract
1 x grade 3 egg, beaten	1 standard	1 medium
6 x 15ml level tbsp cold milk	6 tbsp	9 tbsp

1 Well grease with melted fat a $1\frac{1}{4}$l capacity pudding basin (2pt or American 5 cup). Pour syrup into base.
2 Sift flour into bowl. Add suet and sugar. Toss ingredients with fingertips.
3 Using a fork, mix to a soft batter with vanilla, egg and milk. Stir briskly without beating.
4 Spoon into prepared basin. Cover with cling film, making 2 slits in it with scissors to prevent it from 'ballooning-up' in oven.
5 Cook 4 to $4\frac{1}{2}$ minutes or until pudding rises to top of basin.
6 Take out of oven, remove film and invert pudding on to a plate. Serve portions with cream or custard.

Note: despite the remarkably short cooking time, the pudding is well done and the texture is exceptionally light and spongy.

Steamed jam suet pudding (Serves 4 to 5)

Substitute jam (American preserves) for same amount of syrup.

Christmas pudding (Each pudding serves 4–6)

Ingredients	Imperial	American
150g plain flour	5oz	$1\frac{1}{4}$ cups
25g cocoa powder	1oz	3 level tbsp
3 x 5ml level tsp mixed spice	3 level tsp	$4\frac{1}{2}$ level tsp
175g fresh white breadcrumbs	6oz	3 cups
225g soft brown sugar (dark variety)	8oz	1 cup
225g shredded suet	8oz	$1\frac{1}{3}$ cups
575g mixed dried fruit	$1\frac{1}{4}$lb	4 cups
125g mixed chopped peel	4oz	$\frac{3}{4}$ cup
finely grated rind of 1 small orange	1 small orange	1 small orange
4 x grade 3 eggs	4 standard	4 medium
3 x 15ml level tbsp black treacle	3 level tbsp	4 level tbsp dark molasses
150ml Guinness or other dark beer	$\frac{1}{4}$pt	$\frac{5}{8}$ cup
2 x 15ml tbsp milk	2 tbsp	3 tbsp

1 Well grease 4 x 1pint (575ml or $2\frac{1}{2}$ American cups) pudding basins.
2 Sift flour, cocoa and spice into bowl. Add crumbs, sugar, suet, fruit, mixed peel, and orange rind. Toss thoroughly by running fingers through ingredients.
3 Using a fork, mix to a slackish consistency with eggs, treacle, beer and milk. Stir briskly without heating.
4 Divide equally between prepared basins and cover with cling film. Make 2 slits in each covering of film to prevent it from 'ballooning-up' in oven. Cook puddings individually. Allow 5–6 minutes cooking time, and 5–6 minutes resting time, before turning out of basins and serving.

Genoese sponge sandwich Microwave 'baking' gives a light texture and even rising; the speed of cooking surely compensates for the absence of the traditional 'browning'. (Recipe page 102)

5   Leave in basins for 5 minutes before turning out on to warm plates and cutting into portions. Serve with cream, custard or brandy butter.

Notes: despite the remarkably short cooking time, the pudding has a deliciously fruity, mature flavour and characteristic dark colour.

Leftovers should be wrapped in greaseproof paper (American waxed paper) and then in aluminium foil, and stored in a well-ventilated larder or pantry. If space permits, the pudding can be kept in the refrigerator. To reheat, cut pudding into slices, stand on individual plates and reheat in the microwave for about 1 to $1\frac{1}{2}$ minutes, depending on thickness.

Baked jam pudding (Serves 6)

Ingredients	Imperial	American
3 x 15ml level tbsp jam	3 level tbsp	$4\frac{1}{2}$ level tbsp preserves
175g self-raising flour	6oz	$1\frac{1}{2}$ cups
75g butter or margarine	3oz	$\frac{3}{8}$ cup
75g castor sugar	3oz	$\frac{3}{4}$ cup
finely grated peel of 1 medium lemon	1 medium lemon	1 medium lemon
2 x grade 3 eggs	2 standard	2 medium
3 x 15ml tbsp milk	3 tbsp	$4\frac{1}{2}$ tbsp

1   Brush with melted butter or margarine an oval pie dish of $1\frac{1}{2}$l capacity ($2\frac{1}{2}$pt or American $6\frac{1}{4}$ cups). Cover base with jam (American preserves).
2   Sift flour into a bowl. Rub in butter or margarine finely. Add sugar and lemon peel. Toss ingredients over and over with fingertips.
3   Using a fork, mix to a soft batter with unbeaten eggs and the milk. Stir briskly without beating.
4   When smooth and well-combined, spread evenly over jam. Cook, uncovered, 7 to 8 minutes or until well-risen. At this stage, the top should look almost dry.
5   Remove from oven and leave to rest 5 minutes. Turn out on to a hot dish and serve with cream or custard.

Note: 1 teaspoon vanilla essence (American vanilla extract) may be used instead of lemon peel.

Bananas in rum (Serves 4)

Ingredients	Imperial	American
50g butter	2oz	$\frac{1}{4}$ cup
2 x 15ml level tbsp soft brown sugar (dark variety)	2 level tbsp	3 level tbsp
2 x 15ml tbsp dark rum	2 tbsp	3 tbsp
$\frac{1}{2}$kg 4 bananas	1lb	4 medium

1 Place butter in fairly shallow dish. Melt, uncovered, in microwave 1 to $1\frac{1}{2}$ minutes. Stir in sugar and rum. Cook 1 minute. Stir.
2 Peel bananas. Add to dish and baste with rum syrup. Cook, uncovered, 4 minutes. Half turn dish after 2 minutes.
3 Serve hot with whipped cream or vanilla ice cream.

Easy raspberry mousse (Serves 6 to 8)

Ingredients	Imperial	American
15g gelatine	$\frac{1}{2}$oz	1 envelope
2 x 15ml tbsp cold water	2 tbsp	3 tbsp
1 can raspberries, about 410g	14oz	$1\frac{3}{4}$ cups
3 x grade 3 eggs, separated	3 standard	3 medium
3 x 15ml level tbsp castor sugar	3 level tbsp	$4\frac{1}{2}$ level tbsp
150ml or $1\frac{1}{2}$dl whipping cream	$\frac{1}{4}$pt	$\frac{5}{8}$ cup

1 Tip gelatine into basin. Add water. Leave 2 minutes to soften. Melt 1 to $1\frac{1}{2}$ minutes in microwave.
2 Stir in syrup from can of raspberries, egg yolks and sugar. Beat thoroughly. Leave in the cold until just beginning to thicken and set.
3 Beat egg whites to a stiff snow. Whip cream until thick. Fold egg whites, cream and two-thirds of the raspberries into the jellied mixture. Use a metal spoon and work until mixture is smooth and evenly combined.
4 Transfer to 1 large bowl or individual dishes. Refrigerate until firm and set. Decorate with extra whipped cream, reserved raspberries and finely chopped walnuts just before serving.

Notes: do not freeze.
Canned loganberries may be used instead of raspberries.
If mixture looks on the insipid side, fold in a few drops of red food colouring with the egg whites and cream.

Summer fruit cocktail (Serves 8)

Ingredients	Imperial	American
350g fresh gooseberries	12oz	about $1\frac{1}{2}$ cups
2 x 15ml tbsp water	2 tbsp	3 tbsp
125g castor sugar	4oz	$\frac{1}{2}$ cup
$\frac{3}{4}$kg fresh strawberries	$1\frac{1}{2}$lb	about $2\frac{1}{2}$ cups
225g fresh raspberries	$\frac{1}{2}$lb	about $1\frac{1}{4}$ cups

1 Top and tail gooseberries. Put into fairly deep glass or pottery dish. Add water. Cover with lid or cling film. (If using film, make slits in it with scissors to prevent it from 'ballooning-up' in oven.)
2 Cook 5 minutes, half turning dish once. Remove from oven and uncover. Add sugar and stir until dissolved.
3 Add washed and hulled strawberries and raspberries. Gently turn over and over until all the fruits are well-combined. Cover. When completely cold, chill lightly in the refrigerator. Serve with softly whipped cream or ice cream.

Notes: do not freeze.
For a luxury touch, stir 2 to 3 tablespoons Cointreau or Grand Marnier into the cold fruit cocktail.

Orange syrup dessert cake (Serves 8 to 10)

Ingredients	Imperial	American
75g castor sugar	3oz	$\frac{3}{8}$ cup
150ml or $1\frac{1}{2}$dl water	$\frac{1}{4}$pt	$\frac{5}{8}$ cup
1 x 15ml level tbsp finely grated orange peel	1 level tbsp	$1\frac{1}{2}$ level tbsp
2 x 15ml tbsp Cointreau or Grand Marnier	2 tbsp	3 tbsp

Cake

200g plain flour	7oz	$1\frac{3}{4}$ cups
$\frac{3}{4}$ x 5ml level tsp soda bicarbonate	$\frac{3}{4}$ level tsp	$1\frac{1}{8}$ level tsp
50g butter	2oz	$\frac{1}{4}$ cup
425ml or 4dl natural yogurt	$\frac{3}{4}$pt	$1\frac{1}{2}$ cups
125g castor sugar	4oz	$\frac{1}{2}$ cup
2 x grade 3 eggs	2 standard	2 medium
1 x 5ml tsp lemon juice	1 tsp	$1\frac{1}{2}$ tsp

Decoration

150ml or $1\frac{1}{2}$dl whipped cream	$\frac{1}{4}$pt	$\frac{5}{8}$ cup
2 medium sliced oranges	2 medium	2 medium

1 For syrup, place sugar, water and orange peel in glass or pottery dish. Stir well to combine. Heat, uncovered, in microwave until boiling. Boil, uncovered, 3 minutes. Stir. Cool 5 minutes. Stir in liqueur. Leave on one side.

2 For cake, sift together flour and soda. Melt butter 2 minutes in microwave. Combine butter with yogurt and sugar. Beat in eggs, one at a time. Stir in lemon juice.

3 Using a fork, gradually work yogurt mixture into dry ingredients. When batter is smooth and evenly combined, pour into a well-buttered 30cm (12in) square glass or pottery dish.

4 Cook 12 minutes, giving dish a quarter turn after every 3 minutes. Remove from oven. Coat, while still hot, with syrup. Cool completely then chill 1 or 2 hours in refrigerator. Decorate with whirls of whipped cream and orange slices before serving.

Note: do not freeze.

Peaches and cream sherry trifle (Serves 6 to 8)

Ingredients	Imperial	American
1 jam-filled swiss roll	1	1 jelly roll
3 x 15ml tbsp sweet sherry	3 tbsp	4½ tbsp
¼kg canned peach slices	1 x 1lb can	2 cups
2 x 15ml level tbsp custard powder	2 level tbsp	3 level tbsp vanilla-flavoured cornstarch
2 x 15ml level tbsp castor sugar	2 level tbsp	3 level tbsp
575ml or 6dl cold milk	1pt	2½ cups
150ml or 1½dl double cream	¼pt	⅝ cup heavy cream
1 x 15ml level tbsp toasted coconut	1 level tbsp	1½ level tbsp

1 Thinly slice swiss roll and arrange over base and halfway up sides of fairly shallow glass serving bowl.

2 Moisten with sherry and a little peach syrup. Top with two-thirds of the peach slices.

3 To make custard, place custard powder and sugar into deepish dish. Blend smoothly with a little milk. Stir in rest of milk.

4 Cook 8 minutes or until smooth and thickened, stirring thoroughly at the end of every minute.

5 Pour over trifle and leave until cold and set. Before serving, decorate attractively with whipped cream, remaining peach slices and toasted coconut.

Note: do not freeze.

Chocolate mousse (Serves 4)

Ingredients	Imperial	American
125g plain chocolate	4oz	4 squares
25g butter	1oz	⅛ cup
4 x grade 4 eggs (room temperature)	4 standard	4 medium
1 x 5ml tsp vanilla essence	1 tsp	1½ tsp vanilla extract

1 Break up chocolate and put into basin with butter. Melt 2 to 3 minutes, uncovered, in the microwave.

2 Stir in egg yolks and vanilla. Beat whites to a stiff snow and, using a metal spoon, fold into chocolate mixture.

3 When smooth and evenly combined, transfer to 4 individual dishes or wine glasses. Refrigerate until firm.

4 Before serving, decorate with cream and/or chocolate vermicelli.

Chocolate coffee mousse (Serves 4)

Make as above but omit vanilla. Instead add 2 x 5ml level teaspoons (2 level teaspoons or American 3 level teaspoons) of instant coffee powder or granules to the chocolate and butter before putting into the microwave.

Chocolate brandy mousse (Serves 4)

Make as chocolate mousse but omit vanilla. Instead add 4 x 5ml teaspoons (4 teaspoons or American 6 teaspoons) brandy.

Note: do not freeze any of the above mousses.

10 Cakes

The majority of cakes respond very well to being 'baked' in a microwave and the speed of cooking alone must surely be ample compensation for the absence of traditional browning. The texture of all the cakes given in this section is light and even, the flavour is, in my opinion, just as good as if the cakes were baked in a conventional oven, and they all have a heartening tendency of rising evenly without doming, cracking or sinking. Further, with a dusting of icing or confectioner's sugar over the top, I challenge anyone to tell the difference.

You will notice I have suggested lining all dishes for cakes with cling film: my reasons for this are twofold. Firstly, it eliminates washing up almost completely. Secondly, the cake can easily be lifted out of the dish by the film without being inverted; useful when one is dealing with cakes which are characteristically light in texture and easily damaged by the wires of a metal cooling rack. Should you, however, decide to make a cake on the spur of the moment and find you have run out of film, brush the dish lightly with melted butter or margarine then dust with flour. Alternatively, line base and sides in the traditional way with greased greaseproof paper. Why film at all? Pure convenience. It cannot be used if baking in the conventional way because the prolonged heat of the oven would affect it adversely. In a microwave, on the other hand, the cooking time is brief and the microwaves emitted from the magnetron penetrate plastic materials without causing them any harm or damage (see Introduction, page 10).

To prevent dryness, most cakes made in a microwave usually have more liquid added to them than if they were being made in a conventional oven. Therefore, the batter may appear on the wet side. The exceptions are fatless sponges and genoese cakes with a basic recipe of 25g (1oz or ¼ American cup) plain flour, the same amount of castor sugar and 1 egg.

Please do not be surprised if, when you take the cake out of the oven, the top still looks tacky and

Chocolate walnut cake with cream   Cook for only six-and-a-half or seven minutes. (Recipe page 103)

fractionally undercooked. This is quite in order and, after the cake has been standing for 15 minutes or so, the distribution of heat from within will be sufficient to cook the cake completely and give you a drier-looking top.

Where cakes are concerned, there are three warning bells I have to sound to protect you from failure and myself from complaints. *Do not use metal tins* but keep to glass, ceramic, pottery and rigid plastic. *Do not overcook* by even 2 or 3 minutes or the outside of the cake will dry and harden and you will be confronted with a giant biscuit rather than a cake. *Do not lose patience* and invert the cake on to a cooling tray as soon as it has come out of the oven or the top (still tacky perhaps) could well sink into the wires of the tray, resulting in a surface with deep and jagged lines.

All cakes can be deep-frozen. Those with decorations should be frozen unwrapped until completely hard and then wrapped securely in heavy-duty cling film or aluminium foil.

Sponge cake (Cuts into 6 portions)

Ingredients	Imperial	American
3 x grade 3 eggs, room temperature	3 standard	3 medium
75g castor sugar	3oz	$\frac{3}{8}$ cup
75g plain flour, sifted twice	3oz	$\frac{3}{4}$ cup

1   Using cling film, line a round, straight-sided glass or pottery dish of $18\frac{3}{4}$cm ($7\frac{1}{2}$in) in diameter. The depth should be about 10cm (4in). Press film well against base and sides of dish to smooth out wrinkles. Those which remain will leave minimal impression on cake.
2   Beat eggs and sugar together until they treble in volume and are as thick as softly whipped cream. At this stage, the mixture should be very pale in colour. Add flour.
3   Using a large metal spoon, slowly and gently flip the mixture over and over, making sure edge of spoon cuts across base of bowl frequently so that no unmixed flour is left behind.
4   When smooth and evenly combined, pour into

prepared dish. Cook 4 minutes uncovered.
5   Remove from oven and leave to rest 10 minutes before lifting carefully out of dish on to a wire cooling rack.
6   Remove cling film and leave until completely cold before dusting with castor or sifted icing sugar and cutting into wedges.

Note: this cake is excellent as an accompaniment to hot stewed fruit. It can also be split in half horizontally, filled with either butter cream or whipped cream and jam and then dusted with sifted icing sugar.

Genoese sponge (Cuts into 8 portions)

Ingredients	Imperial	American
4 x grade 3 eggs, room temperature	4 standard	4 medium
125g castor sugar	4oz	$\frac{1}{2}$ cup
50g butter	2oz	$\frac{1}{4}$ cup
125g plain flour	4oz	1 cup

1   Using cling film, line a round, straight-sided glass or pottery dish of $18\frac{3}{4}$cm ($7\frac{1}{2}$in) in diameter. The depth should be about 10cm (4in). Press film well against base and sides of dish to smooth out wrinkles. Those which remain will leave minimal impression on cake.
2   Beat eggs and sugar together until they treble in volume and are as thick as softly whipped cream. At this stage, the mixture should be very pale in colour.
3   Place butter in cup and melt in microwave for 1 minute. Sift flour twice.
4   Gently spoon flour over whisked eggs and sugar then pour butter, down side of bowl, in a slow and steady stream.
5   The next bit is tricky and should be carried out *slowly*. Using a large metal spoon, gently flip mixture over and over, making sure edge of spoon cuts across base of bowl frequently so that no unmixed flour and butter are left behind.
6   When smooth and evenly combined, pour gently into prepared dish. Cook $5\frac{1}{2}$ to 6 minutes uncovered. About halfway through, the mixture will rise to the top

of the dish but falls to a depth of about 5cm (2in) towards the end of its cooking time.

7 Remove from oven and leave to rest 10 minutes before lifting carefully out of dish on to a wire cooling rack.

8 Remove cling film and leave until completely cold before dusting with castor or sifted icing sugar and cutting into wedges.

Genoese sponge sandwich (Cuts into 8 portions)

Cut cold cake in half horizontally. Sandwich together with whipped cream and jam. Dust top with sifted icing or castor sugar.

Lemon genoese sponge gâteau (Cuts into 8 portions)

Follow recipe for genoese sponge but whisk eggs and sugar with finely grated peel of 1 small lemon. When completely cold, cut cake in half horizontally. Sandwich together and coat top and sides with 275ml or 3dl ($\frac{1}{2}$pt or American $1\frac{1}{4}$ cups) double cream (American heavy cream), sweetened to taste with sugar. Press flaked and toasted almonds against sides then decorate top with pieces of jellied lemon slices coated with sugar.

Chocolate walnut cake (Cuts into 8 to 10 portions)

Ingredients	Imperial	American
200g self-raising flour	7oz	$1\frac{3}{4}$ cups
25g cocoa powder	1oz	3 level tbsp
125g butter or margarine	4oz	$\frac{1}{2}$ cup
125g soft brown sugar		
(dark variety)	4oz	$\frac{1}{2}$ cup
50g chopped walnuts	2oz	$\frac{1}{2}$ cup
1 x 5ml tsp vanilla essence	1 tsp	$1\frac{1}{2}$ tsp vanilla extract
2 x grade 3 eggs		
(room temperature)	2 standard	2 medium
6 x 15ml tbsp cold milk	6 tbsp	9 tbsp

1 Using cling film, line a round, straight-sided glass or pottery dish of $18\frac{3}{4}$cm ($7\frac{1}{2}$in) in diameter. The depth should be about 10cm (4in). Press film well against base and sides of dish to smooth out wrinkles. Those which remain will leave minimal impression on cake.

2 Sift flour and cocoa powder into bowl. Rub in butter or margarine finely. Add sugar and nuts. Toss ingredients over and over with fingertips.

3 Using a fork, mix to softish batter with vanilla, beaten eggs and milk. Stir briskly without beating.

4 Spoon evenly into prepared dish and cook, uncovered, until mixture reaches about halfway up the dish and shrinks slightly away from sides. Allow between $6\frac{1}{2}$ and 7 minutes.

5 Remove from oven and leave to rest about $\frac{1}{4}$ hour before lifting or turning out of dish on to a wire cooling rack. Remove cling film and leave cake until completely cold before sprinkling top with sifted icing sugar and cutting into wedges.

Chocolate walnut layer (Cuts into 10 to 12 wedges)

Cut cold cake twice horizontally. Layer together with 275ml or 3dl ($\frac{1}{2}$pt or American $1\frac{1}{4}$ cups) double cream (American heavy cream) beaten until thick with castor sugar and vanilla essence (American vanilla extract) to taste. Cover top with remaining cream, then stud with halved walnuts.

Mocha walnut cream (Cuts into 10 to 12 wedges)

Make butter cream by creaming together 150g (5oz or $\frac{5}{8}$ American cup) unsalted and softened butter with 225g (8oz or $1\frac{1}{2}$ American cups) sifted icing or confectioner's sugar. When light and fluffy, beat in 3 x 5ml level teaspoons instant coffee powder ($4\frac{1}{2}$ level American tablespoons) dissolved in 3 x 15ml tablespoons ($4\frac{1}{2}$ American teaspoons) warm milk. Cut cold cake twice horizontally then sandwich together with butter cream. Cover top with rest of butter cream, ridge with a fork then dust top lightly with drinking chocolate. For a more elaborate gâteau, make double the quantity of coffee butter cream. Use cream both to sandwich layers together and also to spread over top and sides of cake. Press finely chopped walnuts against sides and add a ring of chocolate buttons around top edge.

Cream crowned walnut cake

Swirl or pipe top of cake with 125ml or 1½dl (¼pt or American ⅝ cup) sweetened whipped cream. Decorate with walnuts.

Coffee cake (Cuts into 8 to 10 portions)

Ingredients	Imperial	American
250g self-raising flour	8oz	2 cups
6 x 5ml level tsp instant coffee powder	6 level tsp	9 level tsp
125g butter or margarine	4oz	½ cup
125g soft brown sugar (dark variety)	4oz	½ cup
2 x grade 3 eggs	2 standard	2 medium
5 x 15ml tbsp cold milk	5 tbsp	7½ tbsp

1 Using cling film, line a round, straight-sided glass or pottery dish of 18¾cm (7½in) in diameter and about 10cm (4in) deep. Press film well against base and sides of dish to smooth out wrinkles. Those which remain will leave minimal impression on cake.
2 Sift flour and coffee powder into bowl. Rub in butter or margarine finely. Add sugar. Toss ingredients over and over with fingertips.
3 Using a fork, mix to a softish batter with beaten eggs and milk. Stir briskly without beating.
4 Spoon evenly into prepared dish and cook, uncovered, until mixture reaches about halfway up the dish and shrinks slightly away from sides. Allow between 6½ and 7 minutes.
5 Remove from oven and leave to rest about ¼ hour before lifting or turning out of dish on to a wire cooling rack. Remove cling film and leave cake until completely cold before sprinkling top with sifted icing sugar and cutting into wedges.

Coffee cream gâteau

Cut cold cake in half horizontally. Sandwich together with 250ml or 3dl whipped cream (½pt or American 1¼ cups heavy cream) sweetened to taste with sifted icing sugar and flavoured with either a few teaspoons dark rum or extra coffee powder. Spread rest of cream over top and sides. Decorate top with whole hazelnuts.

Ginger and orange cake (Cuts into 8 to 10 portions)

Ingredients	Imperial	American
225g self-raising flour	8oz	2 cups
1 x 5ml level tsp ground ginger	1 level tsp	1½ level tsp
125g butter or margarine	4oz	½ cup
125g soft brown sugar (dark variety)	4oz	½ cup
grated peel of 1 medium orange	1 medium orange	1 medium orange
50g stem ginger, finely chopped	2oz	2oz
1 x 15ml tbsp ginger syrup	1 tbsp	1½ tbsp
2 x grade 3 eggs, room temperature	2 standard	2 medium
5 x 15ml tbsp cold milk	5 tbsp	7½ tbsp

1 Using cling film, line a round, straight-sided glass or pottery dish of 18¾cm (7½in) in diameter. The depth should be about 10cm (4in). Press film well against base and sides of dish to smooth out wrinkles. Those which remain will leave minimal impression on cake.
2 Sift flour and ground ginger into bowl. Rub in butter or margarine finely. Add sugar, grated orange peel and chopped ginger. Toss ingredients over and over with fingertips.
3 Using a fork, mix to a softish batter with ginger syrup, beaten eggs and milk. Stir briskly without beating.
4 Spoon evenly into prepared dish and cook, uncovered, until mixture reaches about halfway up the dish and shrinks slightly away from sides. Allow between 6½ and 7 minutes.
5 Remove from oven and leave to rest about ¼ hour before lifting or turning out of dish on to a wire cooling rack. Remove cling film and leave cake until completely cold before sprinkling top with sifted icing sugar and cutting into wedges.

Iced ginger and orange cake (Cuts into 8 to 10 portions)

If preferred, cover cake with glacé icing made by mixing 175g (6oz or 1 American cup) sifted icing or confectioner's sugar with sufficient strained orange juice to form a thickish icing. Spread quickly over top of cake, allowing icing to trickle down sides. Leave until set before cutting.

Lemon cherry cake (Cuts into 8 to 10 portions)

Ingredients	Imperial	American
125g glacé cherries, halved	4oz	⅔ cup
250g self-raising flour	8oz	2 cups
125g butter or margarine	4oz	½ cup
125g castor sugar	4oz	½ cup
grated peel of 1 small lemon	1 small	1 small
2 x grade 3 eggs	2 standard	2 medium
½ x 5ml tsp vanilla essence	½ tsp	¾ tsp vanilla extract
5 x 15ml tbsp cold milk	5 tbsp	7½ tbsp

1 Using cling film, line a round, straight-sided glass or pottery dish of 18¾cm (7½in) in diameter. The depth should be about 10cm (4in). Press film well against base and sides of dish to smooth out wrinkles. Those which remain will leave minimal impression on cake.

2 Wash cherries to remove syrup and towel dry. Sift flour into bowl. Rub in butter or margarine finely. Add cherries, sugar and lemon peel. Toss ingredients over and over with fingertips.

3 Using a fork, mix to a softish batter with beaten eggs, vanilla and milk. Stir briskly without beating.

4 Spoon evenly into prepared dish and cook, uncovered, until mixture reaches about halfway up the dish and shrinks slightly away from sides. Allow between 6½ and 7 minutes.

5 Remove from oven and leave to rest about ¼ hour before lifting or turning out of dish on to a wire cooling rack. Remove cling film and leave cake until completely cold before sprinkling top with sifted icing sugar and cutting into wedges.

Farmhouse cake (Cuts into 8 to 10 portions)

Ingredients	Imperial	American
250g self-raising flour	8oz	2 cups
125g butter or margarine	4oz	½ cup
125g soft brown sugar (dark variety)	4oz	½ cup
125g raisins	4oz	¾ cup
50g chopped mixed peel	2oz	⅓ cup
1 x 5ml tsp vanilla essence	1 tsp	1½ tsp vanilla extract
2 x grade 3 eggs	2 standard	2 medium
5 x 15ml tbsp cold milk	5 tbsp	7½ tbsp

1 Using cling film, line a round, straight-sided glass or pottery dish of 18¾cm (7½in) in diameter. The depth should be about 10cm (4in). Press film well against base and sides of dish to smooth out wrinkles. Those which remain will leave minimal impression on cake.

2 Sift flour into bowl. Rub in butter or margarine finely. Add sugar, raisins and peel. Toss ingredients over and over with fingertips.

3 Using a fork, mix to a softish batter with vanilla, eggs and milk. Stir briskly without beating.

4 Spoon evenly into prepared dish and cook, uncovered, until mixture reaches about halfway up the dish and shrinks slightly away from sides. Allow between 6½ and 7 minutes.

5 Remove from oven and leave to rest about ¼ hour before lifting or turning out of dish on to a wire cooling rack. Remove cling film and leave cake until completely cold before sprinkling top with sifted icing sugar and cutting into wedges.

Chocolate brownies (Cuts into about 16 pieces)

Ingredients	Imperial	American
50g plain chocolate	2oz	2 squares bitter chocolate
75g butter	3oz	⅜ cup
175g soft brown sugar (dark variety)	6oz	¾ cup
2 x grade 3 eggs	2 standard	2 medium
150g plain flour	5oz	1⅛ cup
¼ x 5ml level tsp baking powder	¼ level tsp	½ level tsp
1 x 5ml tsp vanilla essence	1 tsp	1½ tsp vanilla extract
2 x 15ml tbsp cold milk	2 tbsp	3 tbsp

1 Brush with melted butter the base and sides of a glass or pottery dish measuring 25 x 16¼ x 5cm in depth (10 x 6½ x 2in).

2 Break up chocolate and put into basin with butter. Melt in microwave for 2 minutes. Stir thoroughly to mix. Beat in brown sugar and eggs and continue to beat until mixture is smooth and evenly combined.

3 Add flour sifted with baking powder, vanilla and

milk. Stir mixture gently with a large metal spoon to form a smooth batter.

4 Spread evenly into prepared dish and cook until mixture rises slightly in dish and top is covered with characteristic broken bubbles. Allow 7 minutes.

5 Cool in dish 10 minutes, dust top with sifted icing sugar, cut into pieces and cool on a wire rack.

Chocolate nut brownies

Add 4 x 15ml tablespoons (4 tablespoons or 6 American tablespoons) finely chopped walnuts at the same time as the sugar. Allow 1 minute longer cooking time.

Note: brownies are typically American and are rich, sweet and good keepers if pieces are stored in an airtight tin.

Blackcurrant cheesecake (Cuts into 8 to 10 portions)

Ingredients	Imperial	American
75g butter	3oz	⅜ cup
175g crushed digestive biscuits	6oz	1½ cups crushed Graham crackers
2 x 5ml level tsp castor sugar	2 level tsp	3 level tsp
½kg Philadelphia cream cheese (room temperature)	1lb	2 large packets
75g castor sugar	3oz	⅜ cup
2 x grade 3 eggs	2 standard	2 medium
2 x 5ml tsp vanilla essence	2 tsp	3 tsp vanilla extract
about ½kg, can blackcurrant pie filling	about 1lb	2 cups

1 Melt butter for 2 minutes in 20cm (8in) glass flan dish about 3¾cm (1½in) deep. Stir in biscuit crumbs and sugar. Press evenly against base and sides of dish.

2 To make cheese filling, beat cheese until smooth with next three ingredients. In the absence of an electric beater, use a rotary whisk.

3 Pour over biscuit crumb base. Cook 12 minutes, giving dish a quarter turn every 3 minutes.

4 Leave until cool then spoon blackcurrant filling over top. Chill 1 hour before serving.

Note: this cake is not suitable for freezing.

Coconut ice drops (Makes 27)

Ingredients	Imperial	American
150ml or 1½dl sweetened condensed milk	¼pt	⅝ cup
225g desiccated coconut	8oz	2⅔ cups
red and green food colourings to tint	to tint	to tint

1 Combine condensed milk and coconut. Divide mixture into three parts. Leave one part plain. Colour second part pink with a few drops of red colouring and colour third part green.

2 Using damp hands, make 9 balls from each part. (Total of 27 balls.)

3 Stand, 9 at a time, on base of oven first lined with paper towels. Cook 1½ minutes. Cool on a wire rack. Store in an airtight tin when cold.

Note: do not freeze.

Sultana cup cakes (Makes 12)

Ingredients	Imperial	American
125g self-raising flour	4oz	1 cup
50g butter or margarine	2oz	¼ cup
50g castor sugar	2oz	¼ cup
2 x 15ml level tbsp sultanas	2 level tbsp	3 level tbsp
1 x grade 3 egg	1 standard	1 medium
2 x 15ml tbsp cold milk	2 tbsp	3 tbsp

1 Sift flour into bowl. Rub in butter or margarine finely. Toss in sugar and sultanas.

2 Mix to a soft batter with unbeaten egg and milk, fork-stirring briskly without beating.

3 Spoon equal amounts into 12 paper cake cases. Arrange, 6 at a time, in a ring on floor of microwave. Cook 2 minutes. Remove from oven.

4 Cool on a wire rack. Sift icing sugar over tops before serving and store in an airtight tin.

Note: the cakes are suitable for deep freezing. Icing sugar should be sifted over the top after cakes have thawed.

Chocolate cup cakes (Makes 12)

Ingredients	Imperial	American
110g self-raising flour	3½oz	just under ½ cup
15g cocoa powder	½oz	1½ level tbsp
50g butter or margarine	2oz	¼ cup
50g soft brown sugar	2oz	¼ cup
25g chopped toasted almonds or walnuts	1oz	¼ cup
1 x grade 3 egg	1 standard	1 medium
2 x 15ml tbsp cold milk	2 tbsp	3 tbsp

1   Sift flour and cocoa powder into bowl. Rub in butter or margarine finely. Toss in sugar and nuts.

2   Mix to a soft batter with unbeaten egg and milk, fork-stirring briskly without beating.

3   Spoon equal amounts into 12 paper cake cases. Arrange, 6 at a time, in a ring on floor of microwave. Cook 2 minutes. Remove from oven and cool on a wire rack.

4   Store in an airtight tin when cold.

Note: the cakes are suitable for deep freezing.

Cocoa crackles (Makes about 16)

Ingredients	Imperial	American
75g butter or margarine	3oz	⅜ cup
2 x 15ml tbsp melted golden syrup	2 tbsp	3 tbsp light corn syrup
3 x 15ml level tbsp cocoa powder, sifted	3 level tbsp	4½ level tbsp
3 x 15ml level tbsp castor sugar	3 level tbsp	4½ level tbsp
75g cornflakes	3oz	2 cups

1   Place butter or margarine and syrup in fairly large dish. Melt in microwave 1½ minutes.

2   Take out of oven and stir in cocoa powder and castor sugar.

3   Using a large metal spoon, gently fold in cornflakes. Toss over and over until all the cornflakes are coated with syrup mixture.

4   Spoon into 16 fluted paper cake cases, stand on a flat tray or board and refrigerate until firm and set.

11 Yeast Mixtures

With interest in home-baked bread—and other yeast goods—gathering momentum all the time, microwave oven users will be heartened to know that ½kg (1lb) batches of either white or wholemeal doughs can be proved in the microwave in only 20 to 25 minutes. As though by magic, the dough doubles in size rapidly and evenly; the result of being given precise amounts of microwave energy (15 seconds at a time) followed by equalizing or rest periods of 5 minutes. The combination of short sharp energy bursts, coupled with the resting times, means that warmth is being distributed in a very controlled way through the dough at exactly the right temperature for the yeast to grow and, in turn, leaven the bread.

This problem-free method of coping with yeast mixtures is a tremendous boon to a busy cook and one can confidently leave the dough and the microwave to work successfully together without worrying about drying out (microwave-risen dough is outstandingly well-textured), under or over-proving, and finding that 'traditional warm place'—usually a sink of hot water or the upstairs linen cupboard—where the dough is normally left to rise for anything up to an hour.

A word of advice which I would ask you to heed. Yeast is easily killed and is unable to function satisfactorily as a raising agent if subjected to prolonged and excessive heat. Therefore follow times given in the recipes *as accurately as you can*. This applies whether you are using packeted bread mixes or the recipes given in this section.

Once proven and shaped, yeasted goods should be baked in a conventional oven for the characteristic golden brown finish. The exceptions are soft-crusted rolls and bread, and a fruity malt loaf which has been especially designed for cooking in the microwave. Bread and rolls, etc, which are to be baked in or on tins in a conventional oven, should *not* be proved the second time round in the microwave.

'Potted' brown bread   The risen dough is cooked in a straight-sided dish. (Recipe page 110)

Basic white bread dough

Ingredients	Imperial	American
1 x 5ml level tsp sugar	1 level tsp	1½ level tsp
275ml or 3dl water, room temperature	½pt	1¼ cups
1 x 5ml level tsp dried yeast	1 level tsp	½ envelope active dry yeast
½kg plain flour	1lb	4 cups
½ x 5ml level tsp salt	½ level tsp	¾ level tsp
25g butter or margarine	1oz	⅛ cup

1   In small bowl or cup, mix sugar with ⅓ of the water. Warm in the microwave 30 seconds. Stir in yeast. Leave 7 to 10 minutes or until it begins to activate and bubble.

2   Sift flour and salt into a bowl. Warm in the microwave 30 seconds. Rub in butter or margarine finely.

3   Mix to a dough with the yeast liquid and rest of water. Knead thoroughly until dough is smooth and no longer sticky; about 10 minutes. Shape into a ball.

4   Return dough to clean and well-oiled bowl. Brush top with more oil to prevent a skin from forming. Cover top of bowl tautly with cling film.

5   Warm in the microwave 15 seconds. Rest 5 minutes. Repeat 3 or 4 times or until dough has doubled in size. Use as required.

Basic brown bread dough

Follow recipe given for basic white bread dough using ½ wholemeal plain flour and ½ white plain flour. Use as required.

Microwave bap rolls (soft-crusted) (Makes 16)

On floured surface, divide risen dough into 16 pieces of equal size. Knead into rounds. Place, in rings of 8, on two greased and floured dinner plates. Heat 30 seconds. Leave to rest for 4 minutes. Repeat 2 or 3 times or until baps double in size. Sprinkle with flour. Cook each batch for 3 minutes. Cool on a wire rack.

Microwave soft brown 'loaf-on-a-plate' (Makes 1 flattish round loaf)

On floured surface, knead risen dough lightly into a round of about 2½cm (1in) in depth. Place on a greased and floured dinner plate. Heat 30 seconds. Leave to rest for 4 minutes. Repeat 2 or 3 times until loaf doubles in size. Brush lightly with milk. Sprinkle with wholemeal flour. Bake 4 minutes. Cool on a wire rack.

Microwave 'potted' brown bread (Makes 1 loaf)

On floured surface, knead risen dough lightly then shape to fit well-greased straight-sided dish of 375ml capacity (¾pt or American 2 cups). Heat 30 seconds. Leave to rest for 4 minutes. Repeat 2 or 3 times until loaf doubles in size and reaches top of dish. Brush lightly with milk. Sprinkle with cracked wheat. Cook 5 minutes. Half turn dish. Cook 2 minutes. Leave in dish about 15 minutes before turning out on to a wire cooling rack.

Tin loaf (white) (Makes 1 loaf)

On floured surface, knead risen dough lightly until smooth. Shape to fit a ½kg (1lb) well-greased loaf tin. Place dough in tin. Cover with greased greaseproof paper or greased foil. Leave to rise in a warm place 15 to 20 minutes or until dough reaches top of tin. Brush with beaten egg or milk. Bake in a hot oven preheated to 230°C (450°F), Gas 8. Allow 25 to 35 minutes or until loaf is well-risen and golden brown and has shrunk slightly away from sides of tin. Turn out and cool on a wire rack.

Tin loaf (brown) (Makes 1 loaf)

Make up basic brown bread dough as directed. Shape risen dough as given for white tin loaf. Place in tin. Cover with greased greaseproof paper or greased foil. Leave to rise in a warm place 15 to 20 minutes or until dough reaches top of tin. Brush with beaten egg or milk. Sprinkle with cracked wheat. Bake and cool as white tin loaf.

Lovers' knot dinner rolls (Makes 16)

Make up basic white or brown bread dough as directed. On floured surface, divide risen dough into 16 pieces of equal size. Roll each into a 20cm (8in) long rope. Tie in a knot. Stand on 2 well-greased baking trays. Cover lightly with greased greaseproof paper or greased foil. Leave to rise in a warm place 15 to 20 minutes or until rolls double in size. Brush tops with beaten egg or milk and sprinkle with poppy or caraway seeds. Bake in a hot oven preheated to 230°C (450°F), Gas 8. Allow between 20 and 25 minutes. Cool on a wire rack.

Greek-style pitta bread (Makes 4 'loaves')

Make up basic white bread dough as directed. On floured surface, divide risen dough into 4 equal size pieces. Knead each lightly into a ball. Roll into an oval measuring 30cm (12in) down centre. Dredge lightly with flour. Dampen edges by brushing with water. Fold each in half by bringing top edge (the part furthest away from you) over bottom. Press edges well together to seal. Place on well greased tray and, without further proving, bake 20 to 25 minutes in a hot oven preheated to 230°C (450°F), Gas 8. Place the loaves—which should by now be deep gold and well-risen—on to a wire cooling rack. Leave until cold before splitting and eating either with kebabs or other Greek dishes.

Microwave pizza (Makes 4)

Ingredients	Imperial	American
½kg risen white bread dough (see basic recipe)	1lb	1lb
75g onion	3oz	1 medium
2 medium garlic cloves	2 medium	2 medium
1 x 15ml tbsp oil for frying	1 tbsp	1½ tbsp
150g tomato purée	5oz	1 tube or about ½ cup
50g canned anchovies in oil	2oz	1 small can
125g black olives	4oz	4oz
350g Mozzarella cheese	12oz	12oz or 1 packet

1 On floured surface, divide risen dough into 4 equal size pieces. Knead quickly until smooth. Roll each out into a 20cm (8in) round. Use to cover 4 plates, each 20cm (8in), well-greased and lightly dusted with flour.
2 Heat, one at a time, for 15 seconds. Leave to rest 4 minutes. Repeat 2 or 3 times or until dough doubles in size.
3 Meanwhile, chop onion and garlic finely. Fry fairly gently in the oil, in conventional way, until light gold in colour. Stir in tomato purée and cook 1 minute over low heat.
4 Spread equal amounts over risen pizzas. Top with half the anchovies and one third of the olives. Cover with thin slices of cheese. Arrange rest of anchovies and olives attractively on top.
5 Cook, one at a time, in the microwave for 5 minutes, giving plate a quarter turn after every minute. Serve hot.

Chelsea buns (Makes 9)

Make up basic white bread dough as directed. After proving, turn out on to floured surface and knead lightly until smooth. Roll out into 30 x 22½cm (12 x 9in rectangle. Brush with 25g (1oz or American ⅛ cup) melted butter or margarine then sprinkle with 75g (3oz or American ½ cup) mixed dried fruit, 2 x 15ml level tablespoons (2 level tablespoons or American 3 level tablespoons) mixed chopped peel and 4 x 15ml level tablespoons (4 level tablespoons or American 6 level tablespoons) soft brown sugar. Roll up like a swiss roll, starting from one of the longer sides. Cut into 9 slices. Place, side by side in rows, in a well-greased 17½cm (7in) square tin. Cover with greased greaseproof paper or greased foil and leave in a warm place 15 to 20 minutes or until double in size. Brush with milk, sprinkle lightly with castor sugar and bake in a moderately hot oven preheated to 190°C (375°F), Gas 5. Allow 30 to 35 minutes. Leave in tin 5 minutes then carefully lift out and cool on a wire rack.

Malt loaf (Makes 2 loaves)

Ingredients	Imperial	American
1 x 5ml level tsp sugar	1 level tsp	1½ level tsp
125ml water, room temperature	¼pt	⅝ cup
2 x 5ml level tsp dried yeast	2 level tsp	1 envelope
½kg plain flour	1lb	4 cups
1 x 5ml level tsp salt	1 level tsp	1½ level tsp
4 x 15ml level tbsp sultanas	4 level tbsp	6 level tbsp
4 x 15ml level tbsp malt	4 level tbsp	6 level tbsp
1 x 15ml level tbsp black treacle	1 level tbsp	1½ level tbsp molasses
25g butter	1oz	⅛ cup
Glaze		
125g apricot jam	4oz	6 tbsp apricot preserve
1 x 15ml tbsp water	1 tbsp	1½ tbsp

1 In small bowl or cup, mix sugar with half the water. Warm in the microwave 30 seconds. Stir in yeast. Leave between 7 to 10 minutes or until it begins to activate and bubble.

2 Sift flour and salt into large bowl. Stir in sultanas. Put malt, treacle (molasses) and butter into a small bowl. Heat 1½ minutes in the microwave. Stir well to mix. Add to dry ingredients with yeast liquid and rest of water.

3 Mix to a soft dough, adding a little water if mixture remains on the dry side. Knead thoroughly until dough is smooth and no longer sticky; about 10 minutes.

4 Divide dough into 2 pieces, shape into neat oblongs and place in 2 oblong glass or pottery dishes lined with cling film. Brush both loaves lightly with oil then cover with cling film.

5 Warm in the microwave 15 seconds. Rest 5 minutes. Repeat 3 or 4 more times or until loaves double in size. Uncover.

6 Cook 2 minutes then interchange dishes from right to left. Cook 2 minutes. Turn dishes round from front to back. Cook 2 minutes. Remove from oven.

7 To make glaze, place jam and water in medium-sized bowl and warm 45 seconds in the microwave. Sieve into clean bowl. Cook, uncovered, 4 to 5 minutes or until jam has thickened up sufficiently to coat back of spoon.

8 Remove loaves from dishes and transfer to a wire cooling rack. Using a pastry brush, brush tops with glaze. Leave until cold before slicing.

To refresh bread

Place in a paper bag on a dish covered with a cloth napkin or tea-towel. Heat until you can feel slight warmth on the surface. The bread will then be ready for serving.

To thaw frozen bread

Remove the wrapper to allow the moisture to escape, otherwise bread will become moist and somewhat soggy. Stand on kitchen paper then warm in microwave as given in chart headed 'Convenience Foods' on page 18.

12 Confectionery

The main advantages of sweet-making in a microwave oven are:

1. Speed;
2. No boiling over;
3. No sticky saucepans to clean;
4. Minimal danger of burns;
5. No constant stirring.

Even this small repertoire should suffice for 'Bring and Buy' sales, bazaars, country garden fêtes, home-made Christmas presents and treats for all the family.

Chocolate truffles (Makes 24)

Ingredients	Imperial	American
125g plain chocolate	4oz	4 squares
25g butter	1oz	⅛ cup
1 egg yolk	1	1
350g sifted icing sugar	12oz	1⅞ cup sifted confectioner's sugar
1 x 5ml tsp vanilla essence	1 tsp	1½ tsp vanilla extract
1½ x 15ml tbsp milk	1½ tbsp	2¼ tbsp
desiccated coconut	for coating	for coating
chocolate vermicelli		

1. Break up chocolate and put into basin with butter. Melt in microwave, uncovered, for 2 minutes.
2. Stir in egg yolk, sugar, vanilla and milk. When thoroughly mixed, leave in the cool to firm up slightly. Roll into 24 balls with damp hands.
3. Toss half in coconut and half in vermicelli. Place in paper cases. Leave to harden before eating.

Note: do not freeze.

Chocolate brandy truffles (Makes 24)

Make as above, substituting brandy for the milk. Omit vanilla.

Chocolate orange truffles (Makes 24)

Make exactly as chocolate truffles but add the finely grated peel of 1 small orange with the sugar. Omit vanilla.

Fudge (Makes about ½kg (1lb))

Ingredients	Imperial	American
350g castor sugar	12oz	1½ cups
pinch of salt	pinch	pinch
40g chocolate		
broken into pieces	1½oz	1½ squares
150ml or 1½dl milk	¼pt	⅝ cup
1½ x 15ml tbsp golden syrup	1½ tbsp	2¼ tbsp light corn syrup
25g butter	1oz	⅛ cup
1 x 5ml tsp vanilla essence	1 tsp	1½ tsp vanilla extract

1 Place all ingredients into a large bowl. Cook, uncovered, in microwave about 8 to 10 minutes or until a little of the mixture, poured into a cup of very cold water, forms a soft ball. Depending on oven, the mixture may need 1 or 2 minutes extra cooking time.
2 Stir frequently and check soft ball stage after 6 minutes of cooking and every minute afterwards.
3 Cool ¼ hour then beat until fudge thickens and becomes dull in appearance. Spread into a 17½cm (7in) square buttered dish. Leave until set then cut into squares.

Old-fashioned candy (Makes 350g (12oz))

Ingredients	Imperial	American
50g butter	2oz	¼ cup
350g soft brown sugar	12oz	1½ cups
150ml or 1½dl milk	¼pt	⅝ cup
1 x 5ml tsp vanilla essence	1 tsp	1½ tsp vanilla extract

1 Place butter in fairly large and deep glass or pottery dish. Melt 2 minutes in the microwave. Add all remaining ingredients.
2 Cook, uncovered, for 3 to 4 minutes or until mixture just begins to boil. Remove from oven and stir thoroughly.
3 Return to oven. Cook, uncovered, 8 minutes. Stir about 3 to 4 times. Remove from oven. Beat mixture until it thickens and loses its shine. (You can speed up the process by standing dish in sink containing some cold water.)

4 Spread quickly into a 17½cm (7in) square dish. Leave until hard. Break up into pieces. Store in an airtight container.

Note: do not deep freeze.

Coffee fudge (Makes about 575g (1¼lb))

Ingredients	Imperial	American
75g butter	3oz	⅜ cup
3 x 15ml tbsp sweetened liquid coffee essence	3 tbsp	4½ tbsp
½kg sifted icing sugar	1lb	2½ cups confectioner's sugar
1 x 15ml tbsp double cream or unsweetened evaporated milk	1 tbsp	1½ tbsp

1 Heat butter and coffee essence in deep glass or pottery dish for 2 minutes in the microwave.
2 Gradually work in icing sugar with cream or milk. When smooth and well-combined, beat until creamy.
3 Spread into 17½cm (7in) buttered square dish. Leave in a cool place until set. Cut into squares and keep cool, especially in hot weather.

Coffee nut fudge (Makes about 575g (1¼lb))

Make exactly as above, adding 4 x 15ml level tablespoons (4 tablespoons or American 6 tablespoons) finely chopped walnuts with the cream or milk.

Note: do not freeze either of these fudges.

13 Preserves

The main advantages of making jam, marmalade, chutneys and lemon curd in a microwave are not only speed and ease of cooking, but also safety, coolness and cleanliness. You are unlikely to get a messy saucepan and sticky cooker through the jam, etc, boiling over; nor will you run the risk of burned utensils and fingers. The kitchen will stay cool and steam-free and the whole exercise can be carried out with the minimum of fuss and bother and the maximum of efficiency. The preparation of ingredients remains the same but when a chutney can be cooked in 30 minutes, a lemon curd in five and a dried apricot jam in under an hour, those who in the past have been reluctant to become involved with making preserves may now feel inclined to have a try.

If you compare the microwave recipes with the traditional ones, you will spot one more major advantage—the lack of personal involvement. The preserve will cook quite happily and safely in the microwave, requiring only the occasional stir from you.

To check the setting point of jam and marmalade, pour a little of either on to a cold saucer. Leave 2 minutes. If a skin forms on top which wrinkles when touched, setting point has been reached. For those with sugar thermometers, the temperature should register 110°C (220°F).

Spoon preserve into clean, warm and dry jars. Top immediately with waxed discs. Cover with cellophane tops when completely cold. Label clearly.

To warm and sterilise empty jars, pour a little water into each. Heat in the microwave 2 to 3 minutes, depending on size and thickness. Heat individually. Pour out water. Turn jars upside down to drain. If necessary, wipe dry with paper towels.

Three-fruit marmalade (Yield 2½ to 2¾kg (5 to 6lb))

Ingredients	Imperial	American
2 medium lemons	2 medium	2 medium
2 medium grapefruits	2 medium	2 medium
2 medium oranges	2 medium	2 medium

850ml or 9dl boiling water	1½pt	3¾ cups
2kg preserving or granulated sugar	4lb	8 cups

1   Wash and dry fruit. Cut in half and squeeze out the juice. Reserve.

2   Remove pith and pips and tie in a piece of clean cloth such as muslin. Shred peel according to taste; fine, medium or coarse.

3   Place juice, bag of pith and pips together with the peel into a large mixing bowl. Add one third of the water. Leave to soak 1 hour. Add rest of boiling water. Cover bowl with cling film, making 2 slits in it with kitchen scissors to prevent it from 'ballooning-up'.

4   Cook in microwave, allowing about 20 minutes for fine peel, 25 minutes for medium and 30 minutes for coarse.

5   Uncover and stir in sugar. Cook, uncovered, for approximately 25 to 30 minutes or until setting point is reached. Stir every 5 minutes.

6   To prevent peel from rising in jars, allow marmalade to remain in bowl until a skin forms on top. Stir round, pot and cover.

Note: the cooking time (point 5) is approximate only. The time the marmalade takes to reach setting point will depend very much on the size and age of the fruit and an extra 10 minutes may be necessary.

Ginger and apple marmalade (Yield ½kg (1lb))

Ingredients	Imperial	American
8g root ginger	¼oz	small piece
½kg cooking apples	1lb	2 large or 4 medium
275ml or 3dl boiling water	½pt	2¼ cups
125g preserved ginger, chopped	4oz	about ½ cup

1   Bruise root ginger well by pounding with a rolling pin. Tie in a piece of thin cloth such as muslin.

2   Wash and dry apples. Slice fairly thinly, without peeling or coring. (Both peel and cores help jam to set.)

3   Place bag of ginger and apples into large bowl. Add water. Cover bowl with cling film, making 2 slits in it with scissors to prevent it from 'ballooning-up' in oven. Cook 10 minutes in microwave, half turning dish after 5 minutes.

4   Turn into a sieve lined completely with a piece of thin cloth. (A 'J'-Cloth does admirably.)

5   Press out as much juice as possible. Measure the juice and allow ½kg sugar (1lb or American 2 cups) to every 575ml or 6dl (1pt or American 2½ cups) juice.

6   Place juice and sugar in large basin. Cook, uncovered, 15 minutes in microwave, stirring every 5 minutes. Check for setting point and allow extra time—up to about 5 to 6 minutes—if necessary.

7   Add preserved ginger then leave marmalade to cool for ¼ hour. Pot and cover.

Strawberry jam (Yield just under 3kg (6lb))

Ingredients	Imperial	American
2kg frozen strawberries	4lb	4lb
15g citric acid	½oz	½oz
1¾kg preserving or granulated sugar	3½lb	7 cups

1   Place fruit and citric acid in large mixing bowl made from glass or pottery. Cover with cling film, making 2 slits in it with kitchen scissors to prevent it from 'ballooning-up' in oven.

2   Cook in microwave 15 to 20 minutes when fruit should be very soft. Uncover. Add sugar and stir until dissolved.

3   Cook, uncovered, in the microwave until setting point is reached, stirring and checking for setting every 10 minutes. Allow a total of 45 minutes, although the jam could set sooner depending on strawberries and the particular microwave oven you are using.

4   Cool jam for 20 minutes or until a skin forms on top. Stir round, spoon carefully into clean dry jars and cover.

Note: half quantity will take about 25 minutes to reach setting point. The yield will be about 1½kg (3lb).

Interesting preserves **Infinitely quicker, cooler and easier to make in a microwave—and here are some really different recipes.**

Dried apricot jam (Yield 1kg (2lb))

Ingredients	Imperial	American
225g dried apricots	8oz	8oz
575ml or 6dl water	1pt	2½ cups
1kg preserving or granulated sugar	2lb	4 cups
4 x 15ml tbsp lemon juice	4 tbsp	6 tbsp
25g blanched and split almonds	1oz	about ¼ cup

1 Wash apricots thoroughly. Soak overnight in the water. Tip into large glass or pottery dish. Cook, uncovered, in microwave for 15 to 20 minutes or until fruit is soft. Remove from oven.

2 In separate bowl, combine sugar and lemon juice and warm 2 minutes in microwave. Add to bowl of apricots and stir until sugar has dissolved.

3 Return to microwave. Cook, uncovered, for 5 minutes. Stir well. Cook 10 minutes. Stir well. Cook further 10 minutes or longer until setting point is reached.

4 Stir in almonds then leave jam to stand for 20 minutes or until a skin forms on the surface. Stir round, pot and cover.

Spicy apple and raisin chutney (Yield 1kg (2lb))

Ingredients	Imperial	American
½kg cooking apples	1lb	2 large or 4 medium
125g onion	4oz	1 medium
25g salt	1oz	¼ cup or 3 level tbsp
375ml or 4dl malt vinegar	13 fluid oz	1⅝ cup
225g soft brown sugar	8oz	1 cup
1 large garlic clove	1 large	1 large
225g raisins or sultanas	8oz	about 1½ cups
21g ground ginger	¾oz	2 level tbsp
21g dry mustard	¾oz	2 level tbsp
½ x 5ml level tsp cayenne pepper	½ level tsp	¾ level tsp

1 Thinly slice peeled apples and onion. Place in large glass or pottery bowl. Add salt, vinegar, sugar and crushed garlic clove. Stir well to mix.

2 Cover bowl with cling film, making 2 slits in it with scissors to prevent it from 'ballooning-up' in oven. Cook 20 minutes, half turning dish after 10 minutes.

3 Blend cooked ingredients until smooth in liquidiser goblet. Return to clean bowl. Stir in raisins. Mix together the ginger, mustard and cayenne pepper then work in some of the chutney mixture.

4 Return spices to bowl of chutney, mix thoroughly then cover with cling film. Leave to 'mature' overnight at kitchen temperature. Pot the following day.

Date and apple chutney (Yield just under 2kg (4lb))

Ingredients	Imperial	American
½kg cooking apples	1lb	2 large or 4 medium
½kg dates, roughly chopped	1lb	about 2 cups
125g preserved ginger	4oz	about ½ cup
275g sultanas or raisins	8oz	about 1½ cups
275g soft brown sugar	8oz	1 cup
40g salt	1½oz	4½ level tbsp
575ml or 6dl malt vinegar	1pt	2½ cups

1 Peel, core and slice apples. Place in large glass or pottery dish. Add remaining ingredients and mix well.

2 Cover bowl with cling film, making 2 slits in it with scissors to prevent it from 'ballooning-up' in oven.

3 Bring chutney to boil in the microwave then cook until thick and jam-like in consistency; about ½ hour. Half turn dish after 15 minutes. Pot and cover.

Lemon curd (Makes about ½kg (just over 1lb))

Ingredients	Imperial	American
125g butter	4oz	½ cup
3 x grade 3 eggs	3 standard	3 medium
1 egg yolk	1	1
225g castor sugar	8oz	1 cup
finely grated peel and juice of 3 medium lemons	3 medium lemons	3 medium lemons

1 In medium-sized glass or pottery dish, heat butter in microwave for 3 minutes.

2 Meanwhile, beat together remaining ingredients and stir into melted butter.

3 Cook, uncovered, 5 minutes, stirring well at the end of every minute. When cooked sufficiently, the curd should be thick enough to coat the back of a wooden spoon.

4 Transfer to 2 or 3 small dry jars. Top with waxed discs. Cover when cold.

14 Combination dishes

The dishes in this section demonstrate how a conventional cooker and a microwave oven can be used together to produce an interesting group of sweet and savoury dishes for starters, main courses and desserts.

Quiche Lorraine (Serves 4 to 6)

Ingredients	Imperial	American
20cm baked pastry case	8in	8in baked pie shell
125g bacon, chopped	4oz	about $\frac{1}{2}$ cup
150ml or 1$\frac{1}{2}$dl single cream	$\frac{1}{4}$pt	$\frac{5}{8}$ cup
150ml or 1$\frac{1}{2}$dl cold milk	$\frac{1}{4}$pt	$\frac{5}{8}$ cup
3 x grade 3 eggs	3 standard	3 medium
$\frac{1}{2}$ x 5ml level tsp salt	$\frac{1}{2}$ level tsp	$\frac{3}{4}$ level tsp
nutmeg for sprinkling	for sprinkling	for sprinkling

1 Stand pastry case on a plate. Sprinkle bacon over base of a shallow dish. Cook, uncovered, 2 minutes in the microwave. Use to cover base of pastry case.
2 Beat next four ingredients well together. Strain into pastry case over bacon. Sprinkle with nutmeg.
3 Cook 6 minutes in the microwave, giving plate a quarter turn at the end of every 1$\frac{1}{2}$ minutes. Leave to stand until lukewarm before cutting and serving. Accompany with salad.

Cheese and bacon pie (Serves 4 to 6)

Make exactly as above, using half the amount of bacon. Sprinkle top of pie with 50g (2oz or American $\frac{1}{2}$ cup) grated Cheddar cheese and nutmeg before cooking.

Cheese and mushroom pie (Serves 4 to 6)

Make exactly as Quiche Lorraine but omit bacon. Instead, cover base completely with single layer of sliced mushrooms. Sprinkle top of pie with 50g (2oz or American $\frac{1}{2}$ cup) grated Cheddar cheese and nutmeg before cooking. Garnish with slices of fried mushrooms.

Cheese and tomato pie (Serves 4 to 6)

Make exactly as Quiche Lorraine but omit bacon. Instead, cover pastry base with 2 medium tomatoes, skinned and thinly sliced. Sprinkle top of pie with 50g (2oz or American ½ cup) grated Cheddar cheese and nutmeg before cooking.

Note: do not freeze any of the above pies as the egg custard mixture will separate out.

Cheese and bacon crumble tart (Serves 6 as a main course)

Ingredients	Imperial	American
17½cm baked flan case	7in	7in baked pie shell
125g bacon, chopped	4oz	about ½ cup
125g plain flour	4oz	1 cup
65g butter	2½oz	7½ tbsp
1 x 5ml level tsp dry mustard	1 level tsp	1½ level tsp
½ x 5ml level tsp salt	½ level tsp	¾ level tsp
50g grated Cheddar cheese	2oz	½ cup
175g, 2 tomatoes, sliced	6oz	2 large

1 Stand flan case on a plate. Place bacon in a shallow glass or pottery dish. Cook, uncovered, 2 minutes in the microwave. Arrange over base of flan case.
2 Sift flour into bowl. Rub in butter. Toss in next three ingredients. Sprinkle crumble thickly over bacon. Press down lightly with back of a spoon.
3 Arrange tomato slices round edge then cook flan 6 minutes, uncovered, half turning plate after 3 minutes. Leave to stand 2 or 3 minutes, cut into wedges and serve hot with sauce (see Sauces section) and vegetables to taste. Alternatively serve cold with salad.

Note: this is suitable for deep freezing.

Tuna stuffed pancakes (Serves 8 as a starter; 4 as a main course)

Ingredients	Imperial	American
8 cooked pancakes, each 20cm	8in	8in
275ml or 3dl white sauce		
(see Sauces section)	½pt	1¼ cups
198g canned tuna	7oz	just under 1 cup
1 x 5ml level tsp prepared mustard	1 level tsp	1½ level tsp
1 x 15ml level tbsp finely chopped onion	1 level tbsp	1½ level tbsp
salt and pepper to taste	to taste	to taste

Topping

2 x 15ml tbsp lemon juice	2 tbsp	3 tbsp
150ml or 1½dl soured cream	¼pt	⅝ cup
2 x 15ml level tbsp chopped chives	2 level tbsp	3 level tbsp

1 Arrange pancakes, side by side, on work surface. Into hot white sauce stir drained and flaked tuna, mustard and onion. Season to taste with salt and pepper.
2 Spread equal amounts over pancakes. Roll up. Stand side by side in glass or pottery dish. Moisten with lemon juice. Cover with lid or cling film. (If using film, make 2 slits in it with scissors to prevent it from 'ballooning-up' in oven.)
3 Cook 8 minutes, giving dish a quarter turn after every 2 minutes. Transfer to warm plates and top with soured cream. Sprinkle with chives.

Notes: do not freeze.
For a finer texture, grate onions instead of chopping.

Crêpes Suzette (Serves 4)

Ingredients	Imperial	American
8 cooked pancakes, each 20cm	8in	8in
40g butter	1½oz	3 tbsp
2 x 15ml level tbsp castor sugar	2 level tbsp	3 level tbsp
strained juice of 1 medium orange	1 medium orange	1 medium orange
1 x 5ml level tsp finely grated orange peel	1 level tsp	1½ level tsp
1 x 5ml level tsp finely grated lemon peel	1 level tsp	1½ level tsp
2 x 15ml tbsp Grand Marnier	2 tbsp	3 tbsp
2 x 15ml tbsp brandy	2 tbsp	3 tbsp

1   Fold pancakes into square 'envelopes' by bringing top and side edges to middle.
2   Place butter in large but fairly shallow glass or pottery dish. Melt 1½ minutes in microwave. Add all remaining ingredients except brandy. Stir well to mix. Cook 1½ minutes in microwave. Stir again.
3   Arrange pancakes, in single layer, over base of dish. Baste with sauce mixture. Cook, uncovered, 4 minutes. Half turn dish after 2 minutes and again baste with sauce.
4   Remove from oven. Pour brandy into cup and heat a few seconds in microwave until lukewarm. Tip into ladle, set alight and pour over crêpes. Serve as soon as flames have subsided.

Note: do not freeze.

Coconut party flan (Serves 10)

Ingredients	Imperial	American
23¾cm baked flan case	9½in	9½in baked pie shell
3 x 15ml level tbsp raspberry jam	3 level tbsp	4½ level tbsp
175g self-raising flour	6oz	1½ cups
75g butter	3oz	¾ cup
75g castor sugar	3oz	¾ cup
4 x 15ml level tbsp desiccated coconut	4 level tbsp	6 level tbsp
2 x grade 3 eggs	2 standard	2 medium
1 x 5ml tsp vanilla essence	1 tsp	1½ tsp vanilla extract
4 x 15ml tbsp cold milk	4 tbsp	6 tbsp
Icing		
225g icing sugar, sifted	8oz	1¼ cup confectioner's sugar
lemon juice for mixing	for mixing	for mixing
Decoration		
4 x 15ml level tbsp crushed or grated chocolate	4 level tbsp	6 level tbsp

1   Stand flan case on a large plate. Spread base with jam. To make filling, sift flour into a bowl. Rub in butter finely. Toss in sugar and coconut.
2   Mix to soft batter with eggs, vanilla and milk, stirring briskly without beating. Spread evenly into flan case over jam.
3   Cook, uncovered, in microwave 5 minutes, half turning plate after 2½ minutes. Leave until cold.
4   To make icing, put sugar into a bowl and mix to a stiffish icing with a few teaspoons of lemon juice. Spread over flan. Leave until half set then sprinkle with chocolate. Cut when icing has completely set.

Note: the flan is suitable for deep freezing but should be left un-iced.

Mincemeat crumble pie (Serves 8)

Ingredients	Imperial	American
17½cm baked flan case	7in	7in baked pie shell
225g fruit mincemeat	8oz	8oz
125g plain flour	4oz	1 cup
1 x 5ml level tsp cinnamon	1 level tsp	1½ level tsp
50g butter	2oz	¼ cup
50g soft brown sugar	2oz	¼ cup

1 Stand flan case on a plate. Half-fill with mincemeat. Sift flour and cinnamon into a bowl. Rub in butter.
2 Toss in sugar then sprinkle crumble thickly over mincemeat. Press down lightly with back of spoon.
3 Cook, uncovered, in the microwave 4 minutes, half turning plate after 2 minutes. Leave to stand 5 minutes. Cut into wedges and serve hot with whipped cream or custard.

Note: this is suitable for deep freezing.

Chocolate banana pie (Serves 6)

Ingredients	Imperial	American
17½cm baked pastry case	7in	7in baked pie shell
65g self-raising flour	2½oz	7½ level tbsp
1 x 15ml level tbsp cocoa powder, sifted	1 level tbsp	1½ level tbsp
40g butter	1½oz	4½ level tbsp
40g soft brown sugar	1½oz	4½ level tbsp
1 x grade 3 egg	1 standard	1 medium
1 x 5ml tsp vanilla essence	1 tsp	1½ tsp vanilla extract
2 x 15ml tbsp milk	2 tbsp	3 tbsp
225g, 2 bananas	8oz	2 medium
icing sugar for sprinkling	for sprinkling	confectioner's sugar for sprinkling

1 Stand flan case on a plate. Sift flour into bowl. Add cocoa powder. Rub in butter. Toss in sugar.
2 Mix to softish batter with egg, vanilla and milk. Thinly slice bananas. Use to cover base of flan case. Spread evenly with chocolate mixture.
3 Cook, uncovered, in the microwave for 5 minutes, half turning plate after 2 minutes. Remove from oven. Sift icing sugar over the top, cut into wedges and serve hot with whipped cream.

Note: do not freeze as the bananas will turn black.

Bread and butter pudding (Serves 4 to 6)

Ingredients	Imperial	American
4 large slices white bread, de-crusted	4 large slices	4 large slices
50g butter	2oz	¼ cup
3 x 15ml level tbsp currants	3 level tbsp	4½ level tbsp
4 x 15ml level tbsp castor sugar	4 level tbsp	6 level tbsp
425ml or 4dl milk	¾pt	1½ cups
2 x grade 3 eggs	2 standard	2 medium

1 Spread bread thickly with butter and cut each slice into 4 fingers.
2 Arrange half the fingers in fairly deep glass or pottery dish, bearing in mind that the mixture rises as it cooks. Sprinkle with currants and half the sugar.
3 Arrange rest of bread fingers on top, buttered sides uppermost. Sprinkle remaining sugar over the top.
4 Beat milk and eggs well together. Pour gently into dish over bread, etc. Cook, uncovered, in the microwave, for 3 minutes. Press down bread. Leave to stand 5 minutes. Cook, uncovered, 5 minutes. Leave to stand ¼ hour. Cook, uncovered, a further 3 to 5 minutes until you can see that custard has set.
5 Remove from oven. Leave to stand 5 minutes. Brown top under a hot grill. Serve hot.

Note: do not freeze.

15 Hints and tips

To avoid mishaps, be guided by the instruction book supplied by the manufacturer of your particular model of microwave oven.

To loosen ice cream and jellies (not in metal containers), warm in the microwave up to 45 seconds.

To soften frozen or refrigerated cake icings and frostings, warm in the microwave for 10 to 20 seconds.

To remove plastic film easily from frozen meat, heat in the microwave for a few seconds or until the wrapper looks moist.

To rehydrate apricots and prunes quickly instead of soaking overnight, put washed fruit into a glass or pottery dish. Add enough water just to cover. Cook 7 minutes. Leave to stand up to 5 minutes.

To soften dried fruit such as sultanas or raisins, follow instructions given under apricots and prunes above, but reduce cooking and standing times by half.

To melt syrup or honey which has become crystal-lised through standing, remove metal cap then heat jar in the microwave for 1 or 2 minutes.

To warm baby foods, remove metal caps then heat jars in the microwave. Allow about 45 seconds for 1 jar and up to 2 minutes for 3 jars.

To warm baby lotion or oil—or even plastic bottles of shampoo in the winter—remove cap and heat for about 20 seconds in the microwave.

To remove peach skins easily, heat whole peaches in the microwave for 20 to 30 seconds, depending on size. Stand 10 minutes then slide off skins.

To warm a damp dish cloth to mop up spills more easily, heat in the microwave for 10 to 15 seconds.

To dry damp salt or sugar, heat in the microwave for 20 to 45 seconds, depending on amount. If salt is in a metal drum, spoon on to plate.

To dry damp newspapers, leave in the microwave for 1 or 2 minutes, depending on thickness.

Acknowledgements

I should like to offer my grateful thanks to Valerie Collins, Chief Home Economist with the Tricity & Moffat Cooking Division of Thorn Domestic Appliances (Electrical) Ltd, for her help and guidance and for preparing all the food for the colour pictures used in this book. A thank you, as well, to Pamela Clegg, of *Ideal Home* magazine, for painstakingly cutting out and collecting for me every available article published on the subject of microwave ovens.

Being neither technical nor overly scientific, I am extremely grateful to the microwave oven manufacturers and distributors in the UK for the time they have devoted to me.

For products supplied, I appreciate the generosity of Thorn (Tricity & Moffat) and also: Aluminium Foils Ltd (cling film and roasting bags); Birds Eye; Bowater-Scott; Cornings (Pyrex and Pyroflam); Dewhurst; Kerrygold; Kraft; New Zealand Lamb; Rank Hovis McDougall; Ross; Walls.

Photography by Peter Becket and Derek Butler, Avonmore Studios Ltd.

Line illustrations by Denys Baker.

Index

Numbers in italic type refer to illustrations.
Almonds with trout, *37*, 43
Aluminium foil, 47
American long grain rice, 80
American omelet, 28
Anchovy sauce, 86
Apple sauce, 87
Apples, 'baked' stuffed, 94
Apricot and almond upside-down orange pudding, 91
Artichokes with hollandaise sauce, 76
Aubergine moussaka, 59, *60*
Aubergines, 72
Avocados, 'baked' salmon stuffed, 35

Bacon, *11*, 24
Baked beans on toast, 25
'Baked'
  egg custard, 92
  eggs, 26
  fish, 42
  jam pudding, 96
  salmon stuffed avocados, 35
  stuffed apples, 94
Bananas in rum, 98
Barbecue-style spare ribs, 61
Baskets, 10
Basting sauce, 16
Béarnaise sauce, 87
Beef
  aubergine moussaka, 59, *60*
  Belgian, in beer, 55
  Bourguignon, 54
  curry, 54
  easy chili con carne, 52
  goulash, 55
  'hot-pot', 52
  lasagne, *81*, 83
  lasagne verdi, 83
  meat loaf, 56
  meatballs neapolitan, 52
  potato moussaka, 59
  Scottish-style mince, 51
  shepherd's pie, 51
  spaghetti bolognese sauce, 89
  stew, 51
  traditional mince, 51
Blackcurrant cheesecake, 106
'Boil-in-the-Bag' fish, 42
Bolognese sauce, 89
Braised celery, 76
Bread
  brown, 110
  Chelsea buns, 111
  Greek-style pitta, 111
  lovers' knot dinner rolls, 111
  malt loaf, 112
  microwave bap rolls (soft-crusted), 110
  microwave 'potted' brown, *108*, 110
  microwave soft brown 'loaf-on-a-plate', 110
  tin loaf (brown), 110; (white), 110
Bread and butter pudding, 124
Bread sauce, 86
Breakfast dishes, *11*
Brownies, chocolate, 105; chocolate nut, 106
Browning, basting sauce, 16
Browning dishes, ceramic, 12

Buck rarebit, 25
Buffet gammon, 62
Buttered plaice, 43; sole, 43

Cakes
  blackcurrant cheese, 106
  chocolate brownies, 105
  chocolate cup cakes, 107
  chocolate nut brownies, 106
  chocolate walnut, 103
  chocolate walnut layer, 103
  chocolate walnut with cream, *101*
  cocoa crackles, 107
  coconut ice drops, 106
  coffee, 104
  coffee cream gâteau, 104
  cream crowned walnut, 104
  farmhouse, 105
  genoese sponge, 102
  genoese sponge sandwich, *97*, 103
  ginger and orange, 104
  iced ginger and orange, 104
  lemon cherry, 105
  lemon genoese sponge gâteau, 103
  mocha walnut cream, 103
  sponge, 102
Candy, old-fashioned, 114
Canned condensed soup, 41; spaghetti, 25
Caper sauce, 86
Carrot soup, cream of, 39
Casserole, courgette, 76
Casserole-type meat, 47, 48
Cauliflower cheese, 76
Caviar blinis, mock, 34
Celery, braised, 76
Ceramic browning dishes, 12, 102
Cheese
  and bacon crumble tart, 121
  and bacon pie 120
  and mushroom pie, *33*, 120
  and tomato pie, 120
  cauliflower, 76
  omelet, 28
  macaroni, 82
  sauce, 86
Cheesecake, blackcurrant, 106
Cheesy baked beans on toast *19*, 25
Chelsea buns, 111
Chicken
  cacciatora, 64
  coq au vin, 64
  country captain, 65
  curry with coconut, *57*, 63
  fricassée of, 63
  in creamed goulash sauce, 65
  jumble, 68
  marengo, 64
  roast, *49*
  Spanish-style paella, 67
  vol-au-vents, 32
Chili con carne, 52
Chocolate
  banana pie, 124
  brandy truffles, 113
  brownies, 105
  coffee mousse, 99
  cup cakes, 107
  fudge, 114

  mousse, 99
  nut brownies, 106
  orange truffles, 113
  truffles, 113, *115*
  walnut cake, 103
  walnut cake with cream, *101*
  walnut layer, 103
Chops
  lamb boulangère, 56
  pork sweet-sour, 61
  pork with sauerkraut, 59
  veal, 61
Christmas dinner (prepared plate-meal), 26
Christmas pudding, *27*, 95
Chutney, 116
Chutney, date and apple, *118*, 119
Chutney, spicy apple and raisin, 119
Cling wrap, 10; 100
Cocoa crackles, 107
Cocoa, hot, 24
Coconut ice drops, 106
Coconut party flan, 122
Coffee
  cake, 104
  cream gâteau, 104
  fudge, 114
  leftover, 24
  milky, 24
  nut fudge, 114
Compote of dried fruit, 94
Confectionery
  chocolate brandy truffles, 113
  chocolate orange truffles, 113
  chocolate truffles, 113, *115*
  coffee fudge, 114
  coffee nut fudge, 114
  fudge, 114
  old-fashioned candy, 114
Convenience food
  canned, 21
  frozen cakes and bread, 21, 22, 112
  frozen fish, 20
  frozen individual meals, 20, 21, 22
  frozen meats, 18, 20
Coq au vin, 64
Courgette casserole, 76
Crab toasts, 35
Crackling, 50
Cream crowned walnut cake, 104
Crêpes Suzette, 122
Crumble, fresh fruit, 92
Cucumber and yoghurt soup, chilled, 41
Cupcakes, chocolate, 107; sultana, 106
Curd, lemon, 116, 119
Curried fish pie, 46
Curry
  beef, 54
  chicken, frozen, 22
  chicken with coconut, *57*, 63
Custard 'baked' egg, 92
Cutlets, veal, 62

Date and apple chutney, *118*, 119
Defrost switch, 13, 48
Dehydrated soup mixes, 41
Dinner rolls, 111
Dough
  microwave—risen, 109

white, 109
wholemeal, 109
Dried apricot jam, 119
Dried fruit compote, 94
Duck
    Normandy, 69
    roast with sage and onion stuffing, 68

Éclairs, 17
Egg custard, 'baked', 92
Egg sauce, 86
Eggs
    'baked', 26
    fried, 26
    oeufs en cocotte, 26, 28
    omelet, 26
        American, 28
        aux fines herbes, 28
        cheese, 28
        French, 28
        ham, 28
        mushroom, 28
        Spanish, 29
        tomato, 28
    poached, 26
    scrambled, *11*, 26
Equipment, (*see* Utensils)

Farmhouse cake, 105
Fish
    'baked' salmon stuffed avocados, 35
    buttered plaice, 43
    buttered sole, 43
    crab toasts, 35
    curried fish pie, 46
    haddock with orange nut rice, 43
    kedgeree, 45
    lemon-soused herrings, 43, *44*
    mock caviar blinis, 34
    poached salmon steaks, 45
    prawn stuffed tomatoes, *23*, 34
    prawn vol-au-vents, 32
    prawns provençale, 46
    trout with almonds, *37*, 43
    tuna and artichoke au gratin, 36
    tuna fish pie, 46
    tuna-stuffed pancakes, 121
Flan, coconut party, 122; *see also* Pastry, Pies
Fondue, traditional Swiss, 29
French omelet, 28
French onion soup, 39
Fricassée of chicken, 63; veal, 61
Fried eggs, 26
Frozen food, 8 (*see also* Convenience foods)
Fruit, cocktail, summer, 98
Fruit, fresh, 91; frozen, 90, 92
Fruity malt loaf, 109
Fudge
    coffee, 114
    coffee nut, 114

Gammon, buffet, 62
Gâteau
    coffee cream, 104
    lemon genoese sponge, 103
Genoese
    cakes, 100
    sponge, 102
    sponge gâteau, lemon, 103
    sponge sandwich, *97*, 103
Ginger and apple marmalade, 117
Glass, 9, 102
Goulash, beef, 55
Gratin dauphinoise, 78
Gravy, 84
Greek-style pitta bread, 111

Haddock with orange nut rice, 45
Ham omelet, 28
Ham, party pâté, *30*, 31
Hard eggs, 17
Herrings, lemon-soused, 43, *44*; with artichokes, 76
Hollandaise sauce, *85*, 87; with artichokes, 76
Hot chocolate fudge sauce, *88*, 89
Hot cocoa, 24
'Hot-pot', beef, 52

Ice drops, coconut, 106
Iced ginger and orange cake, 104
Indian (patna) rice, 80

Irish stew, 56
Italian risotto, 82

Jacket potatoes, 74
Jacket potatoes, stuffed, 74, *75*
Jam
    dried apricot, 119
    pudding, 'baked', 96
    strawberry, 117, *118*
    suet pudding, steamed, 95

Kebabs, lamb, 58
Kedgeree, 45
Kidneys in red wine, 62
Kosher meat, 47

Lamb
    aubergine mousspka, 59
    chops boulangère, 56
    Irish stew, 56
    kebabs, 58
    kidneys in red wine, 62
    Persian, 58
    potato moussaka, 59
Lasagne, *81*, 83; verdi, 83
Lemon cherry cake, 105
Lemon curd, 116, 119
Lemon genoese sponge gâteau, 103
Lemon or orange semolina pudding, 95
Lemon-soused herrings, 43, *44*
Liver pâté, 32
Loaf
    fruity malt, 109
    malt, 112
    meat, 56
Lovers' knot dinner rolls, 111

Macaroni
    alla carbonara, 35
    cheese, 82
Malt loaf, 112
Marengo, chicken, 64
Marmalade
    ginger and apple, 117
    three fruit, 116, *118*
Meat
    casserole type, 47, 48
    defrosting, 47, 48, 50
    kosher, 47
    see also Beef, Pork, Veal, etc
Meat loaf, 56
Meatballs neapolitan, 52
Meringues, 17
Metal, 10, 12, 102
Microwave bap rolls (soft-crusted), 110
Microwave pizza, *15*, 111
Microwaves, 7
Milky coffee, 24
Mince, Scottish-style, 51; traditional, 51
Mincemeat crumble pie, 124
Minestrone, *40*, 41
Mocha marshmallow sauce, 89; walnut cream, 103
Mock caviar blinis, 34
Moussaka, aubergine, 59; potato, 59
Mousse
    chocolate, 99
    chocolate brandy, 99
    chocolate coffee, 99
    easy raspberry, 98
Mushroom
    and onion stuffed tomatoes, 34
    omelet, 28
    sauce, 86
    vol-au-vents, 32
Mushrooms
    Romanian style 'braised', 34
    sliced cooked, 25
    whole cooked, *11*, 24
Mustard sauce, 86

Noodles, 80
Normandy duck, 69

Oeufs en cocotte, 28
Old-fashioned candy, 114
Omelets
    American, 28
    aux fines herbes, 28
    cheese, 28

French ,28
ham, 28
mushroom, 28
Spanish, 29
tomato, 28
Onion and sage stuffing, 69
Onion
    sauce, 86
    soup, French, 39
    stuffed tomatoes, and mushroom, 34
'Open' cooked, 50
Orange
    cake and ginger, 104
    cake and iced ginger, 104
    pudding, apricot and almond upside-down, 91
    semolina pudding, 95
    syrup dessert cake, 98

Paddle, 8
Paella, Spanish-style, 67
Pancakes
    crêpes Suzette, 122
    tuna-stuffed, 21
Paper, 10, 47
Parsley sauce, 87
Pasta
    lasagne, *81*, 83
    lasagne verdi, 83
    macaroni alla carbonara, 35
    macaroni cheese, 82
Pastry
    cheese and bacon crumble tart, 121
    cheese and bacon pie ,120
    cheese and mushroom pie, *33*, 120
    cheese and tomato pie, 120
    chocolate banana pie, 124
    coconut party flan, 122
    mincemeat crumble pie, 124
    quiche Lorraine, 120
Pâté
    liver, 32
    party ham, *30*, 31
Patna rice 80
Peaches and cream sherry trifle, 99
Pears in wine, *93*, 94
Peppers, stuffed, 77
Persian lamb, 58
Pies
    cheese and bacon, 120
    cheese and mushroom, *33*, 120
    cheese and tomato ,120
    chocolate banana, 124
    curried fish, 46
    mincemeat crumble, 124
    shepherd's, 51
    tuna fish, 46
Pitta bread Greek-style 111
Pizza, microwave *15*, 111
Plaice, buttered, 43
Plastic, 9, 102
Plate meal, prepared, 26
Plate meal, reheating, 22
Poached eggs, 26
Poached salmon steaks, 45
Pork
    barbeque-style spare ribs, 61
    buffet gammon, 62
    chops, sweet-sour, 61
    chops, with sauerkraut, 59
Porridge, 24
Potato moussaka, 59
Potatoes
    jacket ,74
    stuffed jacket, 74, *75*
'Potted' brown bread, *108*, 110
Pottery and china, 9, 102
Poultry, defrosting, 47, 48, 50; *see also* Chicken
Power control dial, 13
Prawn sauce, 87
Prawn stuffed tomatoes, *23*, 34
Prawn vol-au-vents, 32
Prawns provençale, 46
Preserves
    date and apple chutney, *118*, 119
    dried apricot jam, 119
    ginger and apple marmalade, 117
    lemon curd, 119
    spicy apple and raisin chutney, 119

strawberry jam, 117, *118*
three-fruit marmalade, 116, *118*
Puddings
 apricot and almond upside-down orange, 91
 'baked' egg custard, 92
 'baked' jam pudding, 96
 'baked' stuffed apples, 94
 bananas in rum, 98
 bread and butter, 124
 chocolate banana pie, 124
 chocolate brandy mousse, 99
 chocolate coffee mousse, 99
 chocolate mousse, 99
 Christmas pudding, *27*, 95
 coconut party flan, 122
 compote of dried fruit, 98
 easy raspberry mousse, 98
 fresh fruit crumble, 92
 lemon or orange semolina, 95
 mincemeat crumble pie, 124
 orange syrup dessert cake, 98
 peaches and cream sherry trifle, 99
 pears in wine, *93*, 94
 semolina, 95
 steamed jam suet, 95
 steamed syrup suet, 95
 summer fruit cocktail, 98
Pulse control, 13
Pulse unit, 48

Quiche Lorraine, 120

Raisin chutney, and spicy apple, 119
Rarebit, buck, 25
Rarebit, Welsh, 25
Raspberry mousse, 98
Ratatouille, *71*, 77
Resting times, 8
Ribs, barbecue-style spare, 61
Rice
 haddock with orange nut rice, 43
 Italian risotto, 82
 Scandinavian risotto, *66*, 82
Roast
 chicken, *49*
 duckling with sage and onion stuffing, 68
 pork, *53*
Roasting
 bags, 10, 47, 50
 meat, 50
 poultry, 50
Rolls, dinner, 111; soft-crusted, 110
Romana, veal cutlets, 62
Romanian style 'braised' mushrooms 34

Sage and onion stuffing, 69
Salmon
 steaks, poached, 45
 stuffed avocados, 'baked', 35
Sambals, 54. 63
Sandwich, genoese sponge, *97*, 103
Sauce
 anchovy, 86
 apple, 87
 basic pouring, 87
 basic white, 86
 basting, 84
 Béarnaise, 87
 bread, 86
 caper, 86
 cheese, 86
 egg, 86
 gravy, 84
 Hollandaise, *85*, 87
 hot chocolate fudge, *88*, 89
 mocha marshmallow, 89
 mushroom, 86
 mustard, 86
 onion, 86
 parsley, 87
 prawn, 87
 spaghetti bolognese, 89

Sauerkraut with pork chops, 59
Scandinavian risotto, *66*, 82
Scones, 17
Scottish-style mince, 51
Scrambled eggs *11*, 26
Seasoning, 9, 50
Semolina pudding, 95; lemon or orange, 95
Shepherd's pie, 51
Slimmer's, pâté, 31
Snacks
 bacon rashers, *11*, 24
 baked beans on toast, 25
 buck rarebit, 25
 canned spaghetti, 25
 cheesey baked beans on toast, *19*, 25
 cocoa, hot, 24
 coffee, leftover, 24
 coffee, milky, 24
 mushrooms, sliced cooked, 25
 mushrooms, whole cooked, *11*, 24
 porridge, 24
 standby plate meals, 25
 tomatoes cooked, *11*, 24
 traditional Swiss fondue, 29
 Welsh rarebit, 25
Sole, buttered, 43
Souffles, 17
Soup
 canned condensed, 41
 chilled cucumber and yoghurt, 41
 clear chicken, 38
 cream of carrot, 39
 cream of vegetable, 39
 dehydrated mixes, 41
 easy chicken broth 38
 French onion, 39
 green pea, 39, *79*
 minestrone, *40*, 41
Spaghetti, 80; bolognese sauce, 89
Spanish omelet, 29
Spanish-style paella, 67
Spare ribs, barbecue style, 61
Spicy apple and raisin chutney, 119
Sponge cakes
 genoese, 102
 genoese sandwich, *97*, 103
 lemon genoese gâteau, 103
 sponge cake, 102
Standing times, 8
Starters
 baked salmon stuffed avocados 35
 chicken vol-au-vents, 32
 crab toasts, 35
 liver pâté, 32
 macaroni alla carbonara, 35
 mock caviar blinis. 34
 mushroom and onion stuffed tomatoes, 34
 mushroom vol-au-vents, 32
 party ham pâté, *30*, 31
 prawn stuffed tomatoes, *23*, 34
 prawn vol-au-vents, 32
 Romanian style 'braised' mushrooms, 34
Steamed jam suet pudding, 95
Steamed syrup suet pudding, 95
Stew, beef, 51; Irish, 56
Stirrer blade, 8
Strawberry jam, 117, *118*
Stuffing sage and onion, 69
Sultana cup cakes, 107
Sweet-sour pork chops, 61
Sweets (*see* Confectionery)
Swiss fondue, 29
Syrup dessert cake, orange, 98

Tart, cheese and bacon crumble 121; *see also* Pastry
Three-fruit marmalade, 116, *118*
Tin loaf, brown, 110; white, 110
Tinned food (*see* Convenience food)
Toast
 baked beans on, 25
 canned spaghetti on, 25
 cheesey baked beans on, *19*, 25

Toasts, crab, 35
Tomato and cheese pie, 120
Tomato omelet, 28
Tomatoes
 mushroom and onion stuffed, 34
 prawn stuffed, *23*, 34
Trifle, sherry peaches and cream, 99
Trivet, 50
Truffles
 chocolate, 113, *115*
 chocolate brandy, 113
 chocolate orange, 113
Tuna and artichoke au gratin, 36
Tuna fish pie, 46
Tuna-stuffed pancakes, 121
Turkey epsañol, 68

Utensils
 aluminium foil, 47
 baskets, 10
 ceramic dishes, 12, 102
 cling wrap, 10, 100
 glass, 9, 102
 metal, 10, 12, 102
 paper, 10, 47
 plastic, 9, 102
 plastic spatulas, 10
 pottery and china, 9, 102
 roasting bags, 10, 47, 50
 trivet, 50
 waxed paper, 10
 waxed plates, 10
 wooden bowls and spoons, 10

Veal
 cutlets romana, 62
 fricassée, 61
 piquant chops, 61
Vegetables
 artichokes with hollandaise sauce, 76
 braised celery, 76
 cauliflower cheese, 76
 courgette casserole, 76
 gratin dauphinoise, 78
 jacket potatoes, 74
 mushroom and onion stuffed tomatoes, 34
 mushroom vol-au-vents, 32
 ratatouille, *71*, 77
 Romanian style 'braised' mushrooms, 34
 stuffed aubergines, 77
 stuffed peppers, 77
 stuffed jacket potatoes, 74, *75*
Vegetable cooking times, 72–3
Vol-au-vent
 chicken, 32
 mushroom, 32
 prawn, 32

Walnut cake
 chocolate, 103
 cream crowned, 104
 with cream, *101*
 layer, chocolate, 103
Waxed paper, 10; plates, 10
Welsh rarebit, 25
White bread, 110; dough 109; tin loaf, 110
Wooden bowls, 10; spoons, 10

Yeast
 basic brown bread dough, 110
 basic white bread dough, 110
 Chelsea buns, 111
 Greek-style pitta bread, 111
 lovers' knot dinner rolls, 111
 malt loaf, 112
 microwave bap rolls (soft-crusted), 110
 microwave pizza, *15*, 111
 microwave 'potted' brown bread, *108*, 110
 microwave soft brown 'loaf-on-a-plate' 110
 tin loaf (brown), 110
 tin loaf (white), 110
Yoghurt soup and chilled cucumber, 41
Yorkshire pudding, 17